A very encouraging and enjoyab
and got me praying more than I
Sam Allberry, Associate Minister, S......,
author of Connected and Lifted

'Enjoyment' and 'prayer' are words that are not normally associated together, but after reading You Can Pray you will not be able to separate them! Tim's book is full of helpful insights into how we should pray, why we should pray and what we should pray. It's simple to read, yet not simplistic, as it engages deeply with the biblical text and also with contemporary issues. The book addresses many of the challenges that hinder us from praying and is jam-packed full of encouragement and tips on how we can become great pray-ers.

Having been in full-time Christian ministry for over twenty years, both in Africa and in the UK, I wish this book had been available when I first started out! It is a must-read for anyone who wants to make prayer easy, biblical and God-glorifying.
Andrew Chard, European Director for AIM International

I am so grateful to Tim Chester for writing You Can Pray. It is gracious yet challenging, accessible yet theologically robust. If you've ever wondered why we need to pray, or how to get better at it, this book will help you enormously. In a crowded market, this is one of the few books on prayer I shall recommend unreservedly.
Pete Greig, founding champion of the 24-7 Prayer movement; Director of Prayer for Alpha International; Lead Pastor of Emmaus Road Church, Guildford, UK

You may be thinking, 'not another book on prayer'; so was I. What I found was a book that challenged how I pray and what I pray for. That was a refreshing reminder of the fundamentals of prayer and the end focus of glorifying God, however he chooses to answer our prayers. Whether you've read a lot of books on prayer or none, this is well worth the read.
Charmaine Muir, Minister for Workplace, All Souls, Langham Place, London

YOU
CAN
PRAY

YOU CAN PRAY

Tim Chester

INTER-VARSITY PRESS
Norton Street, Nottingham NG7 3HR, England
Email: ivp@ivpbooks.com
Website: www.ivpbooks.com

First published 2014

British Library Cataloguing in Publication Data
A catalogue record for this book is available from the British Library.

ISBN: 978–1–78359–084–1
ePub: 978–1–78359–085–8
Mobi: 978–1–78359–086–5

Set in Dante 12/15pt
Typeset in Great Britain by CRB Associates, Potterhanworth, Lincolnshire
Printed in Great Britain by Ashford Colour Press Ltd, Gosport, Hampshire

*Inter-Varsity Press publishes Christian books that are true to the Bible and that
communicate the gospel, develop discipleship and strengthen the church for its mission
in the world.*

*Inter-Varsity Press is closely linked with the Universities and Colleges Christian
Fellowship, a student movement connecting Christian Unions in universities and colleges
throughout Great Britain, and a member movement of the International Fellowship of
Evangelical Students. Website: www.uccf.org.uk*

CONTENTS

INTRODUCTION

This book will tell you how you can be a great pray-er.

I realize that's a bold claim.

You may be new to the Christian faith, and prayer just feels weird. You're supposed to close your eyes, and God is somehow there. You're supposed to talk to God, but it can feel a lot like you're talking to yourself.

Or you may have been a Christian for some time. You know how to say a prayer. Yes, you know the right words to use. But still you struggle to pray, to pray as if it mattered. You try to discipline yourself each day, but it can feel very perfunctory – like an item to tick off a list. Or you just never quite get round to it. Perhaps you hear stories of great prayer warriors. Perhaps you resolve to spend more time in prayer. But life happens, and prayer just doesn't happen.

So what does it take to be a great pray-er?

Acquiring the skill of meditation? Hours spent alone with God? A lot more self-discipline than you seem to be able to muster? A jump to a higher level of spiritual living?

There may be merit in some of these. But none will make you a great pray-er.

I used to work hard at my praying. I developed elaborate patterns. I experimented with different spiritual traditions. I tried emptying my mind so I could hear God speaking. I was attentive to my posture and created special spaces for prayer. I lit candles to focus my concentration. I became quite accomplished at different techniques. But I didn't become the great pray-er I longed to be. Indeed, I suspect I often spent so much time fussing about the externals that I didn't do much real praying at all.

The fact is that the secret of great praying has nothing to do with human effort or skill. Plenty of people would like to think it does because they want to make prayer an achievement. They want to be able to think of themselves as great pray-ers.

But, surprising as it may seem, the secret of great praying is this. You need to know three things about God:

1. God the Father loves to hear us pray.
2. God the Son makes every prayer pleasing to God.
3. God the Holy Spirit helps us as we pray.

If you know these three things, then every prayer you pray will be a great prayer.

In preparation for writing this book, I conducted a survey through my blog.[1] One of the things I asked was what questions people had about prayer. Here is a selection of responses:

- 'Do my prayers really make a difference?'
- 'Is prayer more often a therapeutic method that helps us to work through our emotions?'

- 'What's the best way to approach God in prayer? What's an effective prayer?'
- 'How can I grow in my prayer life?'
- 'How can we spur individuals on to better prayer habits? And how can we spur our community on to better prayer?'
- 'I would love to get a behind-the-curtains peak at the inner workings of prayer from God's perspective.'
- 'How can I have better times of extended prayer along with spontaneous prayer throughout the day?'
- 'How do you stop yourself being distracted and letting your mind wander off God?'
- 'I sometimes feel like I'm being selfish if I ask for myself. I know I shouldn't feel that way, but it's hard to overcome.'
- 'Sometimes I don't know what else to say to the Lord. Is it enough just to remember the person or situation before him, or should I put in more effort?'
- 'Does God mind if I can't think what to say?'
- 'I know it's essential for my soul, so why is it so hard?'

I wonder how many of these resonate with you?

The reality is that I'm not a great pray-er. I'm easily distracted. In fact, I don't think there are any great pray-ers at all, with one exception. And that exception is Jesus. But in Jesus and through Jesus, I'm a great pray-er. I pray prayers that God delights to hear and delights to answer. And in and through Jesus you can pray too.

PART 1
WHY PRAYER IS EASY
(HOW WE PRAY)

1. THE FATHER LOVES TO HEAR US PRAY

How do you feel about prayer? Maybe you love praying. You want 'to do business' with God and 'wrestle' in prayer. Or maybe your heart sinks. You think of a wearying sense of duty or boring prayer meetings. Maybe you feel the burden of being expected to do something you find difficult. Who, after all, feels like a great pray-er? Or maybe you fear being exposed.

If you struggle, you're in good company. The disciples weren't sure about prayer either. So they asked Jesus how to pray:

One day Jesus was praying in a certain place. When he finished, one of his disciples said to him, 'Lord, teach us to pray, just as John taught his disciples.'

He said to them, 'When you pray, say:

"Father,
hallowed be your name,

your kingdom come.

Give us each day our daily bread.

Forgive us our sins,

    for we also forgive everyone who sins against us.

And lead us not into temptation.'''

(Luke 11:1–4)

Our Father loves to hear us

Jesus' teaching on prayer begins with the word 'Father'. Prayer starts with the fatherhood of God.

What images come into your mind when you think about praying? Perhaps a monk deep in contemplation. Or a great Christian leader praying beautiful, profound public prayers. Or a prophet like Elijah performing miracles through his prayers. I think of an elderly man in our church when I was a teenager whose prayers were long, eloquent and full of allusions to the Bible. Or friends at university who always seemed to be hearing God speak to them. Whichever it is, it's intimidating!

But Jesus says prayer is like a child asking her father for help. Simple as that.

I can't overstate how important this is. So many books and talks on prayer make prayer a discipline that we need to work on, so we can become good pray-ers. Prayer then becomes something we achieve. But it's not. Prayer is a child asking her father for help – *nothing more, nothing less.*

The disciples ask their question because they see Jesus praying. Jesus has a relationship of intimacy. He is the true Son of God, as Adam and Israel were intended to be. Moreover, he is the eternal Son of God. He has always been in an intimate, close, loving relationship with his Father. He is the one and only Son, eternally begotten of the Father. He speaks only what he hears from his Father and does only what is his Father's will. He honours the Father, and the Father honours him.

All of that is way beyond our experience of God – except that Jesus now invites us to share that relationship. By faith, we're united with Christ. We're 'in' him. His relationship with God becomes our relationship with God. His intimacy with the Father becomes our intimacy with the Father. *The Father will no more reject our prayers than he will reject the prayers of his own Son, Jesus.* Amazing.

Matthew's version of this prayer begins, 'our Father'. It reminds us that this is a corporate prayer. Even when we pray on our own, we do so as part of a family. But this 'our' is not just about you and me. It's about you and Jesus. When we pray 'our' Father, we're praying to the same Father as Jesus.

Imagine Jesus praying as he does in verse 1. You would expect his Father to hear those prayers. Jesus is his only begotten Son and his obedient Son. Yet the Father is as ready to hear your prayers as he was to hear the prayers of Jesus.

In many ways, it's a mistake to focus on prayer itself, as if prayer was some kind of skill to be acquired. We've seen that prayer is the act of a child asking her father for help. And you don't have to teach a child to ask for things! All that a child needs to know is that she is needy and her father loves her. And all you need to know to pray well is that you're needy and your heavenly Father loves you.

Think about how earthly fathers react when their children first speak. They don't go, 'What did you say? "Dada"? It's not "Dada". It's "Father". How can you be so ignorant? Don't talk to me until you've learnt how to speak properly.' No, in my experience, earthly fathers tend to say, 'Did you hear that? She said, "Daddy". She's so amazing.' (And all the while, I'm thinking, 'It just sounded like a gurgle to me!') Most fathers love it when their children talk to them. It may be garbled and inarticulate, but they're thrilled to hear their child speak, especially when they call their name.

When you pray, you may hear a voice accusing you, saying, 'That's not a good prayer. You need to try harder. You need to do better.' *This is the voice of Satan.* Satan is like the grumpy onlooker who remains resolutely unimpressed by the first words of a small child. The difference though is that Satan's intent is far more malign. He never wants you to talk to your Father. Don't listen to Satan. Rather, listen to your heavenly Father who applauds even your faltering, jumbled attempts.

God gave his own Son for this very reason, so that you can call him 'Father', so that you can pray. Prayer is a gift and an opportunity we're given through Christ. It's nothing more and nothing less than a child asking her father for help.

This is how we worship God. Think about all the things you affirm when you come before God as a child asking her Father for help. You affirm the presence of God – he's able to hear you wherever you are. You affirm the power of God – you ask him, because he's able to deliver. You affirm his grace – he welcomes you despite your sin. You affirm his kindness – he receives us as a Father.

Our Father loves to bless us

> Then Jesus said to them, 'Suppose you have a friend, and you go to him at midnight and say, "Friend, lend me three loaves of bread; a friend of mine on a journey has come to me, and I have no food to offer him." And suppose the one inside answers, "Don't bother me. The door is already locked, and my children and I are in bed. I can't get up and give you anything." I tell you,

even though he will not get up and give you the bread because of
friendship, yet because of your shameless audacity he will surely
get up and give you as much as you need.'
(Luke 11:5–8)

Jesus continues his teaching on prayer by telling a parable.
Imagine a Palestinian family sleeping together in their small
home. Suddenly, there's frantic knocking on the door. A
friend has come asking for bread because he's received an
unexpected visitor. In the culture of the time, there was a
strong expectation that generous hospitality should be shown
to visitors. Failure to do so would be a cause of shame. But
most food was prepared daily, and there were no fridges. So
the only resort of the host without food is to beg from
someone else. Hence the late-night call. But the man is
reluctant. His children are sleeping with him, so to get up
would disturb the whole family.

Jesus was talking about a situation his hearers would well
understand. They could appreciate both the desperation of
the man outside and the reluctance of the man inside. They
could imagine the reluctant neighbour hoping the caller
would try somewhere else. But they could also imagine him
conceding to his request. When Jesus says, 'because of the
man's boldness' or 'shamelessness', he could be talking about
the man outside who knocks until he gets an answer. But I
think he's talking about the man inside who answers the
door because he doesn't want to bring shame on the village's
reputation for hospitality.[1]

What is clear is that Jesus is arguing from the lesser to the
greater. He's not saying that God is like a reluctant neighbour
who has to be nagged before he'll do anything for us. No, he's
saying this: If a reluctant human being will give you what you
want out of concern for his reputation, *how much more* will

your loving heavenly Father do so? If a man will answer your
cry even though he's asleep with his family, *how much more* will
he who never sleeps?

God is ready to hear us. Our Father is willing to hear our
prayers. So Jesus applies the parable with a threefold promise
in verses 9–10:

> So I say to you: ask and it will be given to you; seek and you will
> find; knock and the door will be opened to you. For everyone
> who asks receives; the one who seeks finds; and to the one who
> knocks, the door will be opened.

The leader of any nation is surrounded by various levels of
security. Downing Street, the home of the British prime
minister, is protected by iron gates. A policeman stands
outside. Security officers are positioned inside. They travel
everywhere with him. If you want to see him, you will need
an appointment, but only a few people actually get an appointment with the prime minister. His time is too precious
and his security too important. But imagine you're one of
the prime minister's children. The policeman on the door
opens it for you. The secretary lets you in without an
appointment.

That is what it means for us to pray to our Father. Our God
is much more powerful than earthly presidents and prime
ministers. But we can go to him at any time because he's our
Father. We pray to someone who is always willing to listen.

Must we believe to receive?
But does faith in the Father's willingness to bless us mean that
we need to believe God will always give us whatever we ask
for? Or, as one of the respondents to my prayer survey asked,
'Does believing or not believing a specific prayer will be

answered make any difference to whether God answers it or not?' The answer is no. Indeed, a lot of pastoral harm has been caused by people claiming that God will always give us whatever we ask, if only we have enough faith. The implication is that, if God doesn't answer, it's because I lack faith. People's suffering is then compounded by the mistaken belief that it's their own fault for lacking faith.

Of course, we do need faith to pray. Prayer is an expression of faith. We become God's children when we put our faith in Christ. Unbelievers can pray, but our heavenly Father only guarantees to hear the prayers of his children. When we pray, we need to believe that God is a gracious Father who delights to hear our prayers and a sovereign Father who can answer our prayers.

But we don't need faith that God will definitely and specifically give us whatever we ask before our prayers can be effective. In Acts 12, the believers are praying for Peter to be released from prison when, amazingly, Peter himself knocks at the door. God has answered their prayers and sent an angel to escort Peter out of the prison. But no-one believes it's Peter at the door. Clearly they didn't believe God would give the specific thing for which they were praying. But he still did!

Will God the Father give us whatever we ask?

But what about passages that suggest that God will give us whatever we ask when we pray? In Mark 11:22–24, for example, Jesus says,

> Have faith in God . . . Truly I tell you, if anyone says to this mountain, 'Go, throw yourself into the sea,' and does not doubt in their heart but believes that what they say will happen, it will be done for them. Therefore I tell you, whatever you ask for in prayer, believe that you have received it, and it will be yours.

It's important to realize that Jesus is not talking about any old mountain. Mark tells us where Jesus is: on the outskirts of Jerusalem. So 'this mountain' is the temple mount. Jesus has just pronounced judgment on the temple and created a picture of that judgment in his cursing of a fig tree. The temple should have been a house of prayer for the nations, but the nations were excluded by the trading going on in the court of the Gentiles. Now, as Jesus judges the religion represented by the temple, he tells his disciples that *they* will be the new temple, the place where the nations can pray to God and where God promises to answer prayer. If the disciples have faith in Christ, then they will replace the temple and form this new community of prayer.

'I will do whatever you ask.' Surely then this means every prayer is answered if we pray with enough faith? This phrase comes from John 14:13–14 where Jesus says, 'And I will do whatever you ask in my name, so that the Father may be glorified in the Son. You may ask me for anything in my name, and I will do it.' The key is 'so that the Father may be glorified in the Son' and 'in my name'. This is prayer that matches the agenda of Jesus, and his agenda is to glorify his Father. God may, for example, be glorified through a miraculous healing, but he may also be glorified by our patient endurance of illness. We can be confident our Father will answer our prayers for his glory, but we must leave it to him to decide how he will achieve this. True faith trusts our sovereign Father and trusts that he will do what is best. Paul describes how he prayed three times for a problem to be taken away: 'But [the Lord] said to me, "My grace is sufficient for you, for my power is made perfect in weakness." Therefore I will boast all the more gladly about my weaknesses, so that Christ's power may rest on me' (2 Corinthians 12:9). We'll return to the subject of unanswered prayer (a sensitive and sometimes perplexing issue) in chapter 6.

But even as we qualify what Jesus means by these state-ments, we mustn't lose their rhetorical force. When Jesus promised that God will grant us whatever we ask, he didn't 'balance' these statements, argues Paul Miller, because 'we are not balanced'. We're either confident in ourselves or despairing of ourselves, and in both conditions we don't come to God in prayer. So Jesus responds with hyperbole to get us praying.

> Like a parent whose toddler is about to wander off, Jesus is
> yelling, 'My Father has a big heart. He loves the details of your
> life. Tell him what you need and he will do it for you.' Jesus wants
> us to tap into the generous heart of his Father . . . All of Jesus'
> teaching on prayer in the Gospels can be summarized with one
> word: ask.[2]

An indulgent Father?

There are two contrasting dangers into which we can fall. We can think God will give us whatever we want. Wrong. God doesn't pander to our sinful desires. Human fathers don't give their children whatever they ask for – otherwise tooth decay would be rampant! We respond to our children with love and wisdom. And it's the same with our heavenly Father. His response is always loving and, because it's always loving, he sometimes allows hard things in our lives to make us more like Jesus.

An indifferent Father?

But we can go the other way and think that God is trying to trap us or trick us. He can't quite be trusted. He's making life difficult just so he can play with us or test us. Now, the Bible talks about God testing us to refine our faith. But we can also think – wrongly – of God testing us to find us out or trip us

up, a cruel father who says, 'I'm just toughening you up, son.'
Jesus continues:

> Which of you fathers, if your son asks for a fish, will give him a
> snake instead? Or if he asks for an egg, will give him a scorpion?
> If you then, though you are evil, know how to give good gifts to
> your children, how much more will your Father in heaven give
> the Holy Spirit to those who ask him!
> (Luke 11:11–13)

Again Jesus is arguing from the lesser to the greater. If earthly
fathers give good things to their children, *how much more* will
our heavenly Father do so.

Imagine a father playing a practical joke on his child,
laughing cruelly as the egg on his son's plate unfolds into a
scorpion, or the fish turns out to be a snake. God isn't like this.
He's not a practical joker, messing with our heads while he
laughs at us from heaven. His purposes are always good.
He doesn't always give us what we want, but he always gives
us what is good.

The reference to snakes and scorpions in 11:11–13 is an
echo of a verse in the previous chapter of Luke's Gospel.
When the disciples return from the mission Jesus has sent
them on, Jesus says, 'I saw Satan fall like lightning from
heaven. I have given you authority to trample on snakes and
scorpions and to overcome all the power of the enemy;
nothing will harm you' (Luke 10:18–19). Through their
mission, the forces of Satan are being defeated. Now Jesus says
the Father doesn't answer our prayers with snakes and
scorpions. We pray to our Father who is willing to bless us
and who especially wants to bless our missionary endeavours.
When we pray for our Father's help in mission, he gives us
the Holy Spirit. Through our prayers:

- opportunities will open up and people will hear the gospel.
- we will have the power to proclaim boldly, even in the face of ridicule and rejection.
- lives will be changed, marriages restored, addictions broken, neighbourhoods blessed.
- hearts will be melted, and eyes will be opened.
- eternal futures will be decided – those who reject the gospel will be eternally judged, and those who accept it will be eternally saved.

You may already routinely address God as 'Father'. If not, try starting with the words 'My Father' or 'Our Father' *every* time you pray throughout this coming week.

 You can pray

At the end of each chapter you will find a prayer based on a Bible prayer. I've changed a few words (like the pronouns) to turn what is normally a report of a prayer into an actual prayer we can pray. I suggest you do two things with these prayers. First, when you finish reading each chapter, pray the prayer as it is written. Secondly, take each line as a heading for your own prayers. Use each one to shape your requests. You can use most of these prayers to pray for both yourself and other people.

A prayer based on Colossians 1:9–14

> Father God, the Father of our Lord Jesus Christ,
> fill us with the knowledge of your will
> through all the wisdom and understanding that
>   the Spirit gives,
> so that we may live a life worthy of you

and please you in every way:
>   bearing fruit in every good work,
>   growing in the knowledge of you,
>   being strengthened with all power according
>   to your glorious might
>   so that we may have great endurance and patience,
>   and giving joyful thanks to you, our Father.
For you have qualified us to share
>   in the inheritance of your holy people in the kingdom of light.
You have rescued us from the dominion of darkness
and brought us into the kingdom of the Son you love,
in whom we have redemption, the forgiveness of sins. Amen.

2. THE SON MAKES EVERY PRAYER PLEASING TO GOD

What is a good prayer? What makes our prayers effective?

Many contemporary approaches don't help us answer these questions. We're offered Celtic Christianity, Ignition spirituality, contemplative prayer, warfare prayer and so on. And perhaps we move from one to another in search of something that will make prayer easier or deeper or more effective. There's much we can learn from different Christian traditions. But the danger is that we make prayer an achievement on our part or end up feeling even more inadequate than before.

Our prayers are always good prayers

Here's the central idea of this chapter: *our prayers are always good enough because Christ is always good enough*. The achievement in prayer is all Christ's. What makes our prayers effective, as we saw in chapter 1, is Jesus – nothing more and nothing less. We don't have to look beyond him. Nor do we need special techniques, postures, times, methods or styles. The effectiveness of your prayers won't be judged by your morality, your spirituality, your Bible knowledge, the length or the style of your prayers.

These are the very issues Paul was tackling in Colossae:

> Once you were alienated from God and were enemies in your minds because of your evil behaviour. But now he has reconciled you by Christ's physical body through death to present you holy in his sight, without blemish and free from accusation – if you continue in your faith, established and firm, and do not move from the hope held out in the gospel. This is the gospel that you heard and that has been proclaimed to every creature under heaven, and of which I, Paul, have become a servant.
> (Colossians 1:21–23)

Once we could not come before God in prayer because we were enemies. Imagine an enemy soldier trying to see the king of an opposing nation. Imagine him walking across enemy lines, through enemy territory, through the streets of the capital to the palace, past the perimeter guards, through the palace corridors, past the personal bodyguards, to have a word with the king. It just wouldn't happen. He would be arrested or shot a hundred times over before getting there.

The enemies of God have even less chance of seeing him. 'No one may see me and live,' God told Moses (Exodus 33:20). Our God is a consuming fire. If anything tainted by sin were to enter his presence, it would be consumed by his holy glory. And we're not just tainted with sin – we're soaked in it.

No technique, no spirituality, no morality, no method of prayer can overcome this or win us the right to come into God's presence. So prayer is only possible because God himself has made it possible. Colossians 1:22 says, 'But now he has reconciled you by Christ's physical body through death to present you holy in his sight, without blemish and free from accusation.' No-one can see God and live. But now God will present us holy 'in his sight'. Once we were enemies in our minds because of our evil behaviour. Now, by contrast, we are without blemish and free from accusation.

What has happened? Jesus has happened. God has reconciled us 'by Christ's physical body through death'. We have been reconnected to God through a person (Christ's physical body) and an event (his death).

The person of Christ connects us to God

Paul stresses that the human Christ with a physical body is the one who reconciles us to God (Colossians 1:22). But in verses 19–20, Paul says, 'For God was pleased to have all his fullness dwell in him, and through him to reconcile to himself all things.' In these verses, the emphasis is on Christ the divine person: Christ the One in whom all the fullness of deity dwells. Both the humanity and the divinity of Jesus matter.

It is Christ the God-man who reconciles us to God: 'In Christ all the fullness of the Deity lives in bodily form' (Colossians 2:9). As the God-man, he is a complete and sufficient mediator. He truly represents God for he is fully God, and he truly represents humanity for he is fully human. 1 Timothy 2:5 says, 'For there is one God and one mediator between God and mankind, the man Christ Jesus.' You can pray because you have a perfect mediator: Jesus the God-man.

The cross of Christ connects us to God

The event that reconciles us to God is the cross. God was pleased 'through him to reconcile to himself all things, whether things on earth or things in heaven, by making peace through his blood, shed on the cross . . . he has reconciled you by Christ's physical body through death' (Colossians 1:20, 22).

How does this work? Paul expands on Christ's work on the cross in Colossians 2:13–14:

> When you were dead in your sins and in the uncircumcision of your flesh, God made you alive with Christ. He forgave us all our sins, having cancelled the charge of our legal indebtedness, which stood against us and condemned us; he has taken it away, nailing it to the cross.

The image is of a balance sheet. Our in-comings and out-goings are added up, and when the sums are done there is a huge, outstanding debt owed by us to God. It's beyond the ability of any of us to pay it. But, amazingly, this debt is nailed to the cross, and now it reads: 'Paid in full'.

Once we were enemies who couldn't come before God in prayer. But now Jesus our mediator has reconciled us to God. Our prayers are always acceptable, always effective. Through him – nothing more and nothing less.

Dangers ahead

But look again at Colossians 1:22–23: 'He has reconciled you . . . if you continue in your faith, established and firm, and do not move from the hope held out in the gospel.' It's that 'nothing more, nothing less' that's the rub.

The danger is that we move on from the hope held out in the gospel. We think Christ's mediation is not enough – we need to add something: our own holiness, methods, techniques or spiritual experiences.

Paul says something similar in Colossians 2:6–7: 'So then, just as you received Christ Jesus as Lord, continue to live your lives in him, rooted and built up in him, strengthened in the faith as you were taught, and overflowing with thankfulness.' Paul again says, 'continue'. That faith that saved you is the one by which you should continue to live. There's no new teaching; there are no advanced techniques. The Christian life in general – and prayer in particular – is rooted in the gospel, in the mediation of Christ pure and simple.

This was the challenge facing the Colossians. You don't have to read between the lines to realize they are in danger of adding to Christ. This false teaching said that Christ was OK to start the Christian life with, but to continue and grow you needed more advanced spiritualities. The false options of Colossae are sadly still with us today.

The danger of religious rituals

Paul tells the Colossians not to be intimidated by those who teach that religious observance is the route to more effective prayer: 'Do not let anyone judge you by what you eat or drink, or with regard to a religious festival, a New Moon celebration or a Sabbath day. These are a shadow of the things that were to come; the reality, however, is found in Christ' (Colossians 2:16–17). And there are people today who believe the trappings of religion – the rituals, the offices, the saints – are what matter.

These things are not necessarily wrong in themselves, but, if we think we need them along with Christ, then they're idols that rob Christ of his glory. If people can't live without them, then Christ is no longer their mediator. Paul responds by saying,

> In him you were also circumcised with a circumcision not performed by human hands. Your whole self ruled by the flesh was put off when you were circumcised by Christ, having been buried with him in baptism, in which you were also raised with him through your faith in the working of God, who raised him from the dead.
>
> (Colossians 2:11–12)

The danger of spiritual powers

'Do not let anyone who delights in false humility and the worship of angels disqualify you,' says Paul in Colossians 2:18–19. 'Such a person also goes into great detail about what they have seen; they are puffed up with idle notions by their unspiritual mind. They have lost connection with the head.' Again, these issues have not gone away. There are people who make a big deal of angels. Others emphasize warfare prayer, by which they mean naming demons, territorial spirits and addressing prayer to them. They explicitly say this is prayer for an élite – not for inexperienced Christians.

Note how Paul responds. He says Christ is the creator of all things, both in heaven and on earth, visible and invisible (Colossians 1:16). In other words, what counts are not spirits, but Christ their Creator. Christ is 'head over every power and authority' (2:10). Christ has made a public spectacle of the powers and authorities (2:15).

The danger of mystical knowledge

'See to it that no one takes you captive through hollow and deceptive philosophy, which depends on human tradition and the elemental spiritual forces of this world rather than on Christ' (Colossians 2:8). This is insights for the élite, insider knowledge, special techniques. Again, this is still with us today. Sometimes people say we need particular spiritual experiences, or the mystics point to advanced paths in prayer. They offer us deeper prayer, inviting us to climb a spiritual ladder, to move beyond intercession to contemplation, beyond contemplation to silence, beyond silence to mystical communion with God. It all sounds so impressive. But Paul says such people are merely 'puffed up with idle notions' (2:18–19).

'Mystery' was almost certainly a catchphrase of the false teachers. They offered 'mysteries'. 'Spiritualities' might be the modern equivalent. But Paul says knowledge has replaced mystery: 'The mystery that has been kept hidden for ages and generations . . . is now disclosed to the Lord's people. To them God has chosen to make known among the Gentiles the glorious riches of this mystery, which is Christ in you, the hope of glory' (1:26–27). It's out in the open, proclaimed to everyone in the gospel. It's the mystery of 'Christ in you, the hope of glory' (1:27), not special advanced knowledge or spiritual techniques, but Christ in you, Christ your mediator and Saviour.

We need to see the clear distinction between mystical prayer and gospel prayer, for mystical prayer will always attract the devout. So let's highlight its characteristics and contrast them with biblical prayer.[1]

Mystical prayer	Gospel prayer
is a search for communion with God through contemplation	is a simple, passionate response to God's fatherhood
involves progressive states of spiritual consciousness	involves an 'unpretentious simplicity and childlike sincerity of heart'
involves a stilling of the passions	'arises from emotions of great intensity'
includes a discouragement of petitions, especially for earthly goods	includes an encouragement to petition our heavenly Father
sees silence as contemplation uninterrupted by speech	sees silence as a failure of words to express the heart's emotions
believes in a god in which 'the features of the personality begin to fade'	believes God is three persons

Mystical prayer	Gospel prayer
believes union with Christ is attained through spiritual disciplines	believes union with Christ is given through faith
sees union with Christ as the goal of Christian experience	sees union with Christ as the basis of Christian experience

The reason why mystical prayer is attractive is that it presents prayer or spiritual experience as something we can achieve. In reality, as we've seen, the achievement of prayer is all on God's side. In the mystical and contemplative traditions the goal of spirituality is union with Christ, attained through a pattern of spiritual disciplines or a series of spiritual stages. The imagery of a ladder is often used. Biblical spirituality is the exact opposite. Union with Christ is not its goal, but its foundation. It's not attained through disciplines or stages, but given through childlike faith.

Paul says,

> My goal is that they may be encouraged in heart and united in love, so that they may have the full riches of complete understanding, in order that they may know the mystery of God, namely, Christ, in whom are hidden all the treasures of wisdom and knowledge. I tell you this so that no one may deceive you by fine-sounding arguments.
> (Colossians 2:2–4)

Do you want 'the full riches of complete understanding'? Do you want access to 'all the treasures of wisdom and knowledge'? Well, here they are: *in Christ*. Here's the secret of effective praying: Jesus. And it's really no secret at all. You heard it the very first time you heard the gospel.

The danger of spiritual disciplines

'Since you died with Christ to the elemental spiritual forces of this world, why, as though you still belonged to the world, do you submit to its rules: "Do not handle! Do not taste! Do not touch!"?' (Colossians 2:20–21). Again, rules, codes of conduct and spiritual disciplines have not gone away. We're attracted to these things because they make us think, 'If I do all these things, then I can be a great pray-er.' Paul responds to the above verses by saying,

> These rules, which have to do with things that are all destined to perish with use, are based on merely human commands and teachings. Such regulations indeed have an appearance of wisdom, with their self-imposed worship, their false humility and their harsh treatment of the body, but they lack any value in restraining sensual indulgence.
>
> (Colossians 2:22–23)

Religious rituals, spiritual powers, mystical knowledge and spiritual disciplines are all real issues today. People are always attracted to promises of spiritual success, innovative teaching, higher knowledge and deeper experiences. In response, Paul emphasizes the supremacy of Christ, the fullness of revelation in Christ and the sufficiency of Christ for Christian living. In other words, in the gospel of Christ we have enough in order to pray. Christ is enough.

All the above alternatives offer a spirituality of achievement, spirituality for the élite.

When I was younger, I tried all sorts of things to help me pray: I created a special area for prayer in the corner of my room; I used to light candles; I tried various spiritual traditions; I wrote my own liturgies and exercises. None of these things are wrong in themselves. But in the end I was spending all my time thinking about prayer and no time actually praying. I realized that all I needed to pray was Jesus!

But what I also realized was that I was doing all these things so I could become a person known for my godliness. The goal was not talking with my heavenly Father, but becoming a great pray-er. What mattered was my sense that I had achieved some kind of advanced-level spirituality.

For some, these spiritualities of achievement lead to pride. Such people are, as Paul puts it, 'puffed up' (Colossians 2:18). But most of us, I suspect, are not puffed up but intimidated. Paul says it all looks impressive: it has 'the appearance of wisdom' (2:23). But the truth is that when I try contemplation, I think about shopping lists. The result of this intimidation is this: we *don't* pray because we think we *can't*. But biblical spirituality is a spirituality *of grace*. Remember, the dominant image of biblical spirituality is that of a child petitioning its father.

Jesus makes you a great pray-er

If you've ever asked your dad for anything, then you know how to pray. If you didn't have a dad, then the great news is that you have one now. You can come before a heavenly Father because Jesus has led the way. He has opened the door of heaven and reconciled you to God. He makes your prayers great prayers.

Posture, exercises, liturgies, habits, disciplines may be helpful, but none is necessary. There is *nothing* we can do to make our prayers more effective before God. Our prayers are only effective and wholly effective through Christ's work.

Perhaps this morning you found a moment to pray. What happened in that moment? Perhaps you tried to find a quiet spot, but you could still hear the children shouting. You tried to focus on God, but you kept circling back to the problems of your day. You tried to say something, but it sounded rather pathetic. After a couple of minutes your mind had wandered. You gave it another go. You prayed for a couple of friends and asked God to bless the mission of your church. Maybe you weren't sure what to do next. So, feeling a little guilty, you gave up.

All of this may be true, but it is not the whole truth or even the main truth. This is what was really happening in that moment. The Lord of the universe looked on you and saw his child. He thought of his Son. He remembered his death. And so he welcomed you into his presence. You may have been sitting on your sofa, but as you prayed, you stepped into the courts of heaven to stand before the Ancient of Days. You may have felt your sin, but the Father saw only the righteousness of his Son. You may have felt the inadequacy of your prayers, but in your faltering words the Father heard the echo of his Son. All your confused and selfish motives were purged by the blood of Jesus so that your prayers were transfigured into the most beautiful liturgy. As you spoke, the Father's heart filled with joy. The Father gave his Son so that he could enjoy moments like this with you.

Many of us think we are bad pray-ers. Prayer makes us feel guilty. But there's no such thing as bad prayer. *Prayer is not something you can be good or bad at*, not a skill to master or a discipline to practise. It's more like being a passenger in a car. I can choose to get into the car or not. But once I'm in it, I can't claim to be good or bad at being transported along. Only a fool would cry, 'Hey, look at how good I am at "passenging"!' The car does all the work. I just sit there. And in prayer, Jesus has done all the hard work, and I just talk.

So it doesn't matter how long you pray or how eloquent your words are. Jesus makes all your prayers good prayers, makes you a good pray-er. Your prayers are a delight to God the Father. He hears them through his Son. He looks on you in his Son and delights in you. Don't think you must work hard to pray well. Don't feel guilty about not praying for a long time each day. Enjoy the relationship with your heavenly Father that you have in Christ.

This book is not about the steps you can take to become a great pray-er. The message of this book is that you already are a great pray-er in Christ. Through Christ, you can pray.

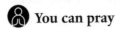 **You can pray**

A prayer based on 2 Thessalonians 1:11–12

> Our God, we pray
>   that you may make us worthy of your calling,
> and that by your power you may bring to fruition
>   our every desire for goodness and
>   our every deed prompted by faith.
> We pray this so that the name of our Lord Jesus
>   may be glorified in us, and we in him,
> according to your grace
>   and the grace of the Lord Jesus Christ. Amen.

3. THE SPIRIT HELPS US AS WE PRAY

I'm what I call 'phone-phobic' – I just hate using the phone. I think it's something about holding disembodied conversations with no body language to help things along. I used to work with a PA who loved talking on the phone. She could ring someone up and within five minutes establish some point of personal contact that would have them eating out of her hand. But I'm not like that. I prefer, if I can, to wait until I see people in the flesh, or I try to persuade my wife to make calls on my behalf. It's worse still if I'm contacting a stranger or asking for help. I always put off those calls until the last minute. There's nothing wrong with my phone; it's just that I'm always reluctant to use it.

Think of prayer as a phone call. The Father is on the other end of the line ready to take the call. Jesus connects us to the Father, and that connection is always reliable. But we still have to pick up the phone and make the call. How will we do that if we think of God as a stranger? Or if we're worried about what to say? This is where the Holy Spirit steps in.

Feeling like God's children

Our salvation is a legal act. Paul talks about Jesus being condemned so that 'the righteous requirement of the law might be fully met in us' (Romans 8:4). This glorious foundation for our salvation means that our standing before God is not dependent on our actions or feelings.

But salvation is more than a legal reality. We're saved for a relationship with God. In Romans 8:29, Paul says that God chose to save us so that his Son 'might be the firstborn among many brothers and sisters'. We become part of the divine family. Jesus is our Brother, and God is our Father. The pinnacle of our salvation is our adoption as God's children. Adoption is the good news of our intimacy, affection, closeness with God.

So that we might know ourselves to be God's children, and so that we can pray like children, God sent his Spirit:

> For those who are led by the Spirit of God are the children of God. The Spirit you received does not make you slaves, so that you live in fear again; rather, the Spirit you received brought about your adoption to sonship. And by him we cry, 'Abba, Father.' The Spirit himself testifies with our spirit that we are God's children.
> (Romans 8:14–16)

Without the Spirit, we wouldn't pray. Do an experiment with me. Every day for a month ask the Queen for something. Wherever you are, say your request out loud to the Queen. I suspect you won't keep it up for a month because it's a futile exercise. Try it now. Say out loud, 'Hello, Your Majesty. Could I have an invitation to Buckingham Palace?' It feels stupid. For one thing, she's not there with you. What's the point of asking for something when the Queen can't hear you? And even if she was in the room with you, her likely response would be: 'Who are you?' Or she would just call security to have you removed. She might well respond to one of her children, but you have no claim on her.

Why doesn't prayer feel like this? The answer is that we have the Holy Spirit. When we pray, we feel connected to the Father, because that's what's happening – the Spirit *is* connecting us to the Father. When we pray, we feel the Father hears us, because the Spirit assures us that he is our Father. If the Spirit wasn't at work in your heart, then you just wouldn't pray. Every time you tried to pray, you would feel like a mad man ranting in the street or a child talking to her imaginary friend.

But we do pray, we can pray, we should pray, because the Spirit assures that God is *our Father* who longs to hear us. The Spirit of God enables us to share the experience of sonship that God the Son experiences. That is a glorious gift of grace. It means confidence, intimacy and joy.

John Bunyan, the author of *Pilgrim's Progress*, wrote a book on praying in the Spirit. He said,

> There is no man nor church in the world that can come to God in prayer, but by assistance of the Holy Spirit . . . If men did see their sins, yet without the help of the Spirit they would not pray . . . There is nothing but the Spirit that can lift up the soul or heart to God in prayer . . . The soul that rightly prays, it must be in and with the help and strength of the Spirit; because it is impossible that a man should express himself in prayer without it.[1]

He explains,

> O how great a task it is, for a poor soul that becomes sensible
> of sin and the wrath of God, to say in faith but this one word,
> 'Father!' . . . O! says he, I dare not call him Father; and hence it is
> that the Spirit must be sent into the hearts of God's people for
> this very thing, to cry Abba, Father: it being too great a work for
> any man to do knowingly and believingly without it.[2]

Help for weak pray-ers

This doesn't always mean an experience of serenity, calm and happiness, unfortunately. Paul continues in Romans 8:17, 'Now if we are children, then we are heirs – heirs of God and co-heirs with Christ, if indeed we share in his sufferings in order that we may also share in his glory.' We will share the Son's experience of glory, but we will also share his experience of suffering.

The word translated 'cry' in Romans 8:15 ('by him we *cry* "*Abba*, Father"') is a strong word. It's the cry a child makes when she's fallen over, when a dog bites her leg, or when she's lost: 'Dad, help, I need you.' It's the kind of cry that makes a father come running.

My nineteen-year-old daughter was looking after a friend's child recently. I was working upstairs when I heard a plaintive, undulating 'Daaad!' in a tone of voice I hadn't heard for many years. I ran downstairs to find that our two-year-old friend had vomited all over my daughter. My independent-minded nineteen-year-old doesn't normally think she needs her dad. But in this situation she was desperate for my help! It's this cry for help from a father that Paul is talking about.

The only time in the Gospels where Jesus says '*Abba*, Father' is in Gethsemane as he sweats blood. '*Abba*, Father' is what you cry when you feel the brokenness of the world. Jesus was about to bear this brokenness on the cross and he cries out, '*Abba*, Father'. And when we feel the brokenness of the world, the Spirit prompts us to cry out, '*Abba*, Father'. Paul goes on to describe the frustration of creation (Romans 8:18–22): 'The whole creation has been groaning as in the pains of child-birth.' Adoption is not a sentimental notion. In the midst of the brokenness of life, the Spirit prompts us to cry out, '*Abba*, Father'.

When we talk about experiencing the Spirit, there are moments of ecstasy, of spine-tingling joy, of thrilling excite-ment. But also, 'the Spirit helps us in our weakness'. The Spirit is near to us in times of distress and confusion. Paul continues:

> In the same way, the Spirit helps us in our weakness. We do not know what we ought to pray for, but the Spirit himself intercedes for us through wordless groans. And he who searches our hearts knows the mind of the Spirit, because the Spirit intercedes for God's people in accordance with the will of God.
> (Romans 8:26–27)

In these verses, we've reached the point where we're so over-whelmed by our problems that we just don't know what to say. Maybe we want to pray, but we don't know where to begin. Maybe we start to pray, but our head is spinning and our thoughts are pulled this way and that. We start to pray to God, but soon find ourselves re-enacting angry conversations or imagining impending disasters. Or maybe we don't want to pray at all. We just want to curl up and wish the world would go away. Yet even in this turmoil of emotions, we can still be truly praying. John Bunyan says, 'The best prayers have often more groans than words: and those words that they have are but a lean and shallow representation of the heart, life, and spirit of prayer.'[3]

What does the Spirit do in those moments? *First, the Spirit helps our prayers*. The word 'helps' in verse 26 has the sense of bearing the burden with us or sharing the load.[4] The Spirit doesn't take over, but joins us in the struggle. It's hard work pushing a car on your own, and often you can't get it moving at all. But if a strong friend joins you and you push together, then it's fairly easy to propel a car (at least along a flat road). On our own, we can't get prayer moving, as it were. But the good news is that the Spirit bears the burden with us. Or imagine feeling too weak to row a boat. You're exhausting yourself and getting nowhere. And then the wind hits the sails. That's how the Spirit helps us in prayer. It's happening even if all you feel is the struggle to pray. The Spirit is not helping us in prayer only when prayer feels easy, but when we can only groan.

Secondly, the Spirit translates our prayers. We pray, but we don't know what to ask, or all we can manage is a heavenward groan. But the Spirit takes our intent and translates it to God. Or he takes our mistaken request and corrects it to God. The result is that 'the Spirit intercedes for God's people in accordance with the will of God' (8:27). The prayers we can't articulate or the requests we get wrong are translated so that they arrive before God as prayer in accordance with his will.

God the Father sees our hearts and perceives the intent in our prayers. Every prayer you pray with good intent is the right prayer to pray – or at least it is when it arrives before God. Charles Spurgeon is reported to have said, 'I thank God that my prayers go to heaven in the revised version.'[5] If you don't know what to say or what to ask, it really doesn't matter. Just pray. Let the Spirit sort out the will of God. Because the Spirit knows what the Father wills, the Spirit prays what the Father wills. And because the Spirit prays what the Father wills, the Father knows what the Spirit prays – even when it's wordless.

You can pray the wrong thing because you pray selfishly. James 4:3 says, 'When you ask, you do not receive, because you ask with wrong motives, that you may spend what you get on your pleasures.' But you can't pray the wrong thing if the desires of your heart are right. Whatever gobble-degook comes out of your mouth or whatever crazy request you ask, any prayer prayed with good intent will be the right prayer.

This is so freeing. You don't have to understand fully the situation so you know the best thing to ask. Nor do you have to work through some mysterious process of discerning God's will before you can pray. Just pray! Sometimes we can feel we need to make suggestions to God. Just pray and leave the rest to the Spirit.

This doesn't mean that we'll always get what we ask for. It's liberating to know that God the Spirit is translating our prayers, and God the Father will answer them with complete wisdom. We might not get what we want or even what we like, but we always get what is good for us. And that good is that we are conformed to the image of God the Son. Paul continues:

> And we know that in all things God works for the good of those who love him, who have been called according to his purpose. For those God foreknew he also predestined to be conformed to the image of his Son, that he might be the firstborn among many brothers and sisters. And those he predestined, he also called; those he called, he also justified; those he justified, he also glorified.
>
> (Romans 8:28–30)

Pray to grow

In these opening chapters, we've seen how:

- God the Father loves to hear us pray.
- God the Son makes every prayer pleasing to God.
- God the Holy Spirit helps us as we pray.

Prayer is the embodiment or outworking of the gospel. We come to the Father through the work of the Son in the power of the Spirit. That statement both summarizes the gospel and describes the practice of prayer. It means we grow as pray-ers not by developing advanced techniques, but by learning to appreciate the gospel more and more. The more we understand the gospel, the better we will pray.

But the opposite is also true. The more we pray, the better we will understand the gospel.

Consider Anna. Anna is a new Christian, and there's still much about Christianity that leaves her confused. But as she spends time with her Christian friends, she hears their prayers and then she herself begins to pray. Previously she assumed prayer was about connecting with some kind of 'life-force'. But now she hears her friends talking to God as a person who can hear what they say. They encourage her to call him 'Father'. They ask for things as if he might do what they ask. They expect him to respond even regarding national and international events. She, too, starts asking God for things. She finds herself acting as if God is everywhere, so he can hear her when she prays. There's a reverence in the way her friends speak to God, but also a freedom. They talk to him without fear. They often end their prayers with the words 'in the name of Jesus', as if Jesus somehow connects them to God.

Think how much Anna is learning every time she prays. Note how much theology is packed into the act of praying:

- the doctrine of the Trinity
- the personhood of its members
- the fatherhood of God
- the grace of God
- the mediation of Christ
- the omnipresence of God
- the sovereignty of God
- human weakness and need
- human responsibility

And this is just the bare act of praying. All this is implied and reinforced before you even give your prayers any content.

Think too how the act of praying corrects our theology.

- You may think of God as unapproachable, but when you pray, you approach him, and the Spirit testifies that he's your Father.
- You may feel your life is a mess or be consumed by anxiety, but the act of praying implies that God can intervene and that he's in control.
- You may think God is distant or that he has abandoned you, but when you pray, you imply that he's with you and hears you.
- You may think of yourself as unworthy, and indeed you are, but in prayer you come before God in the name of Jesus, and his name is sufficient.
- You may think that your future or your ministry depends on you, but when you pray, you imply that it's God's actions that really matter.

As I type, I know that I can move the cursor to the beginning of my document with a combination of keys on my computer keyboard. I could do it now without a moment's reflection.

But here's the odd thing: I can't tell you what that combination of keys is. I would have to sit at a keyboard and let my fingers find the right spot. I do it reflexively, instinctively, intuitively. I've done it so many times, I can now do it without thinking. There are similar patterns of instinctive learning involved in driving a car, playing a musical instrument, navigating the area you live in and so on. Sophisticated levels of knowledge have become second nature through repeated practice.

The same is true of prayer. My list of theological truths implied in the act of praying is the result of reflecting on that act. But I don't reflect every time I pray. Most of the time, I'm not consciously listing out those truths. Yet the act of praying reinforces them. I learn them, just as I've learnt combinations of keys on my computer keyboard. At some point, I found out how to move the cursor to the beginning of a document. But after hours of typing, that knowledge is now embedded in my mind. One of the significant ways in which the truths of the gospel are embedded in our hearts is through the act of prayer.

Traditionally, the church has said: *lex orandi, lex credendi*, that is, what the church prays is what the church believes. It means that you'll see a person's true theology and true priorities emerge in their prayers (or lack of prayers). It means that it's important to have a grace-centred, trinitarian view of prayer, because your praying will shape you. It also means that the act of praying will cause us to grow as Christians. It's not that we have to get in the hours like a trainee using a flight simulator before they're approved as a pilot, but more like spending time with a friend, with the result that we come to know them really well. As we pray, we're learning to live in relationship with the triune God.

So the practice of prayer both implies and shapes theology. We learn that God is in control and that he graciously responds to our requests. We learn to live in relationship with the triune God. Prayer is theology in action. Or, better still, it is theology in relationship.

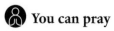 **You can pray**

A prayer based on Romans 15:5–6, 13

> Father, you are the God who gives endurance and
>   encouragement.
> Give us the same attitude of mind towards each other
>   that Christ Jesus had,
> so that with one mind and one voice
> we may glorify you,
>   the God and Father of our Lord Jesus Christ.
>
> Father, you are the God of hope.
> Fill us with all joy and peace as we trust in you,
> so that we may overflow with hope
> by the power of the Holy Spirit. Amen.

PART 2
WHY PRAYER IS DIFFICULT
(WHY WE PRAY)

4. 'I'VE GOT MORE ENJOYABLE THINGS
   TO DO'

If prayer really is easy, then why do we find it so hard?

Because we *do* find it hard. Here's a selection of comments and questions from those who responded to my prayer survey:

- 'Why is it so difficult sometimes?!'
- 'Does it ever get any easier?'
- 'What can I do when it feels like a drudge or a duty?'
- 'Why am I so slow to pray?'
- 'Why don't I cherish prayer more?'
- 'Why is it so hard to make prayer the priority that it should be?'
- 'How can I stop my mind wandering?'

The problem is not with prayer itself. As we've seen already, prayer itself is not hard. We don't find it a struggle because it's difficult to connect with God. We're not like the prophets of Baal who in 1 Kings 18 have to spend all day shouting,

dancing and slashing themselves with swords in a vain attempt
to get through to their god. No, prayer is easy. All the hard
work was done by Jesus at the cross.

Yet your intentions to pray are overtaken by the busy-
ness of life. Or you start praying, but very quickly your
mind is wandering. The main things that stopped people
praying, according to my prayer survey, were in the following
order:

- lack of time
- pride or complacency
- distractions
- laziness and lack of discipline
- unanswered prayer or doubts about its effectiveness
- an inability to focus
- spiritual dryness or a lack of motivation
- sinfulness
- tiredness

Here are some of the things people said:

- 'I feel swamped with work, but I know the real problem
  is that I don't feel dependent on God. When I actually
  pray, I find it ever so helpful, but the perversity of my
  heart makes me forget that!'
- 'Stress and upsets throw me off and make it difficult to
  concentrate.'
- 'My main obstacle to prayer is sin. I'd rather watch the
  news or check email. If I feel dry spiritually, then I don't
  pray.'
- 'Sometimes my problem is not wanting to repent of sin
  or not wanting to ask God to act in some areas, because
  I don't actually want to change.'

- 'As my life got busier and my commute less, my prayer life suffered. I need peace and quiet to pray really effectively and I don't always seek this enough.'
- 'I know I'm blessed when I make time to be with God. Yet I still find it hard to do! But I do believe the Holy Spirit chases us and gently nudges us back into conversation with God, such is his grace.'

Part 1 looked at *how we pray*. These chapters look at *why we pray*. The answer, as we will discover, is twofold. We pray to enjoy the triune God and we pray to ask God to change the world.

Better things to do?

Let me tell you honestly what I think the problem is: *we don't think prayer is worth it. We think there are better things we could be doing.* OK, we don't put it as starkly as this to ourselves, but that is what is going on.

I have a friend who is the leader of a large church in the UK. He spends two hours or more in prayer each day. It's not that he has more hours in a day. It's not that there are twenty-six hours in his day so he has two hours extra for prayer that I don't have. No, the difference is we have different priorities. We all make time for what matters to us. Our real problem is that prayer doesn't really matter to us.

We feel we ought to pray more and assume that the problem is a lack of willpower. So we resolve to get up early, devise a plan, set a target, make a list. But, on their own, these things don't work (Colossians 2:20–23). That's because the problem doesn't ultimately lie with our will. The Bible says that what drives our will is our love or our desire. In the end, we always do what we want. We pursue the priorities of our heart. So the key is to kindle our desire and love for God. That means recognizing that I'm not able, but he is able, so I want to run to him for help. And it means recognizing that he is the source of true delight, so I want to run to him to enjoy his love afresh.

Consider the following:

One thing God has spoken,
    two things I have heard:
'Power belongs to you, God,
    and with you, Lord, is unfailing love.'
(Psalm 62:11–12)

We don't pray because we don't really believe one or both of these two truths: that God is powerful and that God is loving:

- When we doubt God's power, we think of prayer as a waste of time.
- When we doubt God's love, we think of prayer as a dreary duty.

So we think we have better things to do. It's not that we're heretics. If you asked me whether God was good, I would immediately say, 'yes'. But my life tells a different story. I live so much of my life as if God is not good or as if my future depends on me.

When my daughters were young, they couldn't get enough time with their dad. They just loved being with me. We spent many happy hours making things out of Duplo bricks or reading the same stories repeatedly or walking down the street talking about everything we saw. But as they've grown older, they've increasingly found their old dad boring and even embarrassing. Thankfully, they do still have moments when they hang around chatting with their mother and me. But they no longer live for our attention. They still come to us, of course, when they want our help. But they need us less and less as they grow older. And all this is natural and right. Children become adults. In time, there is every likelihood that our daughters will support my wife and me, and we in turn will go to them for help.

But the children of God never stop being children. We never leave home. By all means, let us mature as Christians (Ephesians 4:11–16), but please let us never grow old. Indeed, Christian maturity increasingly involves recognizing and enjoying our status as God's children.

It's when we lose our desire for intimacy with our heavenly Father or our sense of needing his help that our praying becomes dull and lifeless. Prayer becomes difficult when we replace a desire for intimacy and a need for help with a sense of duty.

There's also the danger of focusing too much on prayer itself. Thinking about prayer won't make you want to pray. It's the One to whom we pray that matters. Thinking about the power and love of our Father in heaven is what will give life to our praying. Imagine talking to a loved one on the phone. If all you think about is the phone, then you're not going to have a very good time! If all you think about is the mechanics of prayer, then prayer will be a burden. And all the time, at the other end of the line, is your glorious, gracious heavenly Father.

Why don't we pray more? Because there are other things we'd rather be doing. We just don't find prayer *fun*. We'd rather be watching television, reading a book, meeting with people. Truth be told, we would often rather be cleaning the toilet even. (After all, it doesn't clean itself.) There are some tasks that need to be done. And perhaps praying isn't one of them.

Let's get our bearings for a minute. In this chapter and the next, we're considering two reasons for not praying:

- 'I've got more enjoyable things to do'
- 'I've got more urgent things to do'

We don't enjoy prayer because we misunderstand what it is. Too readily we think of it as an exercise to be performed or a duty to be fulfilled or a skill to be mastered. One of the first things we often tell a new Christian is that they ought to pray each day. So I learn to pray because I'm supposed to. All too easily, this then falls into the category of things like cleaning my teeth, washing my hands, tidying my room. Every now and then, someone asks, 'Are we praying enough?' To which, of course, no-one feels they can answer 'yes'. So we resolve to pray more. Prayer becomes this activity we 'do'. I try to get up earlier. I set a goal of praying for an hour. But I give up after ten minutes. If you think of prayer in these terms, then no wonder you soon begin to think you've got more enjoyable things to do.

Jesus gives us a model for prayer

Luke seems particularly interested in the prayer habits of Jesus. Twice in his Gospel he tells us that Jesus went to 'a solitary' or 'lonely place' (Luke 4:42; 5:16), and three times that Jesus went to a 'mountain' to pray (6:12; 9:28; 22:39). On a couple of those occasions, he tells us that this was Jesus' regular habit (5:16; 22:39). So, for example, in Luke 5:16 we're told, 'Jesus often withdrew to lonely places and prayed.' The concern seems not so much to pray on his own, since sometimes Jesus took disciples with him (Luke 9:28; 22:39–46), but to escape life's distractions and the pressing issues of ministry (Luke 4:42; 5:15–16). Luke describes it as an act of withdrawal.

It's also clear that Jesus was disciplined. He prayed as situations arose, but he also made choices to pray. In Luke 11:1 we read, 'One day Jesus was praying in a certain place. When he finished, one of his disciples said to him, "Lord, teach us to pray."' This suggests that Jesus dedicated specific times to prayer. Jesus says he has prayed ahead of time for Peter who is going to be tested (Luke 22:32). Before appointing the twelve apostles, we're told: 'Jesus went out to a mountainside to pray, and spent the night praying to God' (Luke 6:12–13). So Jesus is disciplined, diligent and intentional about praying.

If Jesus gives us a model for prayer that is disciplined, diligent and intentional, then how does that make you feel? Inspired? But perhaps also intimidated. What are you going to do now? Try to be a better pray-er? More disciplined? Work harder at your praying? Those might all be good things to attempt, but they're not particularly good news. They sound more like a recipe for frustration and guilt.

Jesus gives us so much more than a model for prayer

The good news is that Jesus is doing so much more than simply giving us a model. He came so that we could *enjoy* prayer.

Luke 10:21 says, 'At that time Jesus, full of joy through the Holy Spirit, said, "I praise you, Father, Lord of heaven and earth."' How does Jesus experience joy? It's not self-generated. He has joy 'through the Holy Spirit'. He prays 'through the Holy Spirit'. Now that's exciting. We're not left to pray on our own. Jesus himself, the Son of God, prays with the help of the Spirit. His discipline in prayer is enabled by the Spirit. And the same Spirit is in you if you're a Christian. And notice that Jesus prays: 'Father'. In the next chapter, Jesus invites *us* to call God 'Father' (Luke 11:2).

Then it gets more wonderful still: 'All things have been committed to me by my Father. No one knows who the Son is except the Father, and no one knows who the Father is except the Son' (Luke 10:22). We have a picture of the life of the Trinity. The persons of God know one another, are known by one another, love one another, rejoice in one another, praise one another. The Father praises the Son, and the Son praises the Father in the joy of the Holy Spirit. The Father knows the Son, and the Son knows the Father in the love of the Holy Spirit. Father, Son and Spirit live in mutual love.

Jesus invites us to join in the pleasure of God

But here's the point: Jesus now invites us into that shared life, into the community of divine love. We can call God 'Father' just as he himself calls him 'Father':

> I praise you, Father, Lord of heaven and earth, because you have hidden these things from the wise and learned, *and revealed them to little children*. Yes, Father, for this is what you were pleased to do.
>
> All things have been committed to me by my Father. No one knows who the Son is except the Father, and no one knows who the Father is except the Son *and those to whom the Son chooses to reveal him*.
>
> (Luke 10:21–22, my italics)

The Father is revealing himself to those who come as little children. The Son is revealing the Father to those he chooses. We're being brought into this life of divine love. And *this is God's pleasure*. The Father so delights in his Son that it's his pleasure to see his Son loved. The Son so delights in his Father than it's his pleasure to see his Father praised.

This is what prayer is. It's not us trying to persuade God to be good to us. It's not an achievement. It's a gracious invitation to share the pleasure of the triune God, the delight of the Father in the Son and the Son in the Father through the Holy Spirit. James Torrance says, 'As Christ was anointed by the Spirit in our humanity to fulfil his ministry for us, so we are united by the same Spirit to share his ministry . . . Worship is the gift of participating in the incarnate Son's communion with the Father.'[1]

It's also a gracious invitation to share the purposes of the triune God. Jesus is rejoicing because the disciples' names are written in his book of life (Luke 10:18–20). We're being invited to join, through prayer, the divine mission to defeat Satan and rescue the lost.

Jesus invites us to join in the family of God

> When all the people were being baptised, Jesus was baptised too. And as he was praying, heaven was opened and the Holy Spirit descended on him in bodily form like a dove. And a voice came from heaven: 'You are my Son, whom I love; with you I am well pleased.' (Luke 3:21–22)

John the Baptist is baptizing believers in the River Jordan. Baptism was an act of repentance: these people were saying they had sinned against God and needed a new start, signalling their hope that the Saviour who John said was coming would save them. So it seems odd that Jesus wants to be baptized too. He hasn't sinned and he doesn't need saving. In fact, he is the Saviour!

But Jesus is identifying with us, saying, 'I'm one with these sinful, broken people. They're my people.' Immediately after the baptism, Luke gives us the genealogy of Jesus, which he takes right back to Adam. Jesus is descended from Adam. In other words, he is truly human, one of us.

So what? Look at what happens when Jesus is baptized. The Spirit descends on him, and the Father speaks of him. The Father says, 'You are my Son, whom I love; with you I am well pleased.' Jesus has the anointing of the Spirit and the approval of the Father.

In the Old Testament, these words are spoken to King David's descendants. Adam was the representative of humanity, and his sin led us all into sin and judgment. But God promised that salvation would come through Abraham's descendants. Israel became the representative and hope of humanity. In time, the king became the representative of Israel. So these words mark out Jesus as the representative of Israel and therefore of humanity. And he has God's approval. Jesus is the one who will restore our humanity and reconnect us with God. As Glen Scrivener puts it, 'Jesus joins us in our filth so we can join him in his family.'[2]

It wasn't enough for Jesus to lean down from heaven, as it were, and shout, 'Come up and join us.' What could we do? Jump? No, he comes down and joins *us*, takes on human flesh, becomes one of us. He dies for our sin and rises to give new life. He sends his Spirit so we can be united to him. And if we are united to Christ, then we are in him. Where he is, there we are. And he is participating in the life of the Trinity, part of the divine family. So we, too, participate in the life of the Trinity and are part of the divine family.

God's plan was to make us his children, to give us the same rights as his own Son. But to make us like his Son, he had to make his Son like us: 'In bringing many sons and daughters to glory, it was fitting that God, for whom and through whom everything exists, should make the pioneer of their salvation perfect through what he suffered' (Hebrews 2:10). For us to experience glory, Jesus has to experience suffering. To be qualified as our Saviour, he had to experience what it was to be human: 'Both the one who makes people holy [i.e. Jesus] and those who are made holy [i.e. us] are of the same family. So Jesus is not ashamed to call them brothers and sisters' (Hebrews 2:11). Jesus joined the human family so we could join the divine family.

Jesus leads the choir
Jesus not only joins the family, but the congregation. Hebrews 2:12–13 continues:

> He says,
> > 'I will declare your name to my brothers and sisters;
> > > in the assembly I will sing your praises.'
> And again,
> > 'I will put my trust in him.'
> And again he says,
> > 'Here am I, and the children God has given me.'

The word 'assembly' is the word 'congregation'. Hebrews 12 describes a great heavenly congregation praising God, and we are part of it. When we sing, our voices are heard in heaven. When you sing at St Stephen's or Anytown Christian Fellowship, you're in heaven, joining in the praise of the heavenly choir. You may need to raise your game, because there are angels singing with you when you sing!

Hebrews paints a scene with God surrounded by the congregation of heaven. But here's the question: where is Jesus in this scene? The answer is: he's *with us*. He is on the throne, but also part of the congregation. Don't worry too much about how Jesus can be in two places at once. The focus is on his function, not his location. He's doing two things at once: receiving worship and offering worship. He's leading the singing. Hebrews 2:12 says, 'In the assembly I will sing

your praises', and in verse 13 we read: 'He says, "Here am I,
and the children God has given me."'

We have 'a high priest, who sat down at the right hand of
the throne of the Majesty in heaven, and who serves in the
sanctuary, the true tabernacle set up by the Lord, not by a
mere human being' (Hebrews 8:1–2). Jesus is the God-man.
So he is on the throne *and* leading the worship. He is literally
'a minister of the holy things'. *Jesus* is the one who makes our
worship beautiful to God.

Gareth Malone is an enthusiastic choirmaster who has
turned amateurs into beautiful choirs. Most famously, he took
on a group of military wives. Women who'd never previously
sung in public performed live on television at the Royal Albert
Hall before the royal family. Their single: 'Wherever You Are'
became the UK Christmas number one in 2011.

Jesus is our choirmaster. He didn't sit in heaven, thinking
what a dreadful din those people were making! No, he entered
our world, joined the choir. He trains not our voices, but our
hearts to sing God's praise. He takes our sinful hearts and
transforms them in a beautiful song of praise that is a delight
to God.

But even this does not quite capture what Christ does. It's
not that he trains us to be better pray-ers. If that were the
case, then my prayers might be improving, but they would
still be less than adequate. No, we pray *in him*. His singing
elevates our singing. When I pray, God hears his Son. And
so the Father looks on me and says, 'This is my Son whom
I love; with him I am well pleased.' When I pray, the Father
hears the voice of Jesus. The Reformer John Calvin says,
'For he who prays thus conceives his prayers as from the
mouth of Christ himself, since he knows his own prayer
to be assisted and recommended by the intercession of
Christ.'[3]

Here are some of the comments of the military wives after their performance at the Royal Albert Hall:

- 'I absolutely loved it.'
- 'This is the most emotional, joyful, absolutely fantastic experience of my life.'
- 'Before, we were just military wives, stuck at home with the kids. People are actually hearing us now, and we've got a voice. And that's it. We have a voice now.'

That is how we should feel when we pray. Imagine being one of those wives. You're unknown, stuck at home with the children. You've never sung before. And then for weeks you practise. Finally, you stand on the stage of a packed Royal Albert Hall before a television audience of 6 million. And at the end of your performance the place erupts into applause, and there's not a dry eye in the house. What a moment. What an experience.

That's the experience we enjoy every time we pray. We perform before God himself. And at the end of the performance, he's delighted. By faith, we hear his applause. 'It was the experience of a lifetime,' said one of the wives, 'something I will treasure for ever.' You can say that of *every time* you pray. The difference is this: you get to do it again and again and again.

'We have a voice now.' And that voice reaches up to heaven.

Think Trinity when you pray

My number-one piece of advice for enjoying prayer is, when you pray, '*think Trinity*'. By that I mean a couple of things:

1. Think about the three persons

Pray conscious of each of the three persons of the Trinity. Pray to the Father through the Son in the Spirit. Why does this matter? Because it's easy for us to think we're praying to a 'thing', a god, a force, something up there. We try to imagine God in our minds. But God is invisible. It all seems so abstract. How can we see the invisible God? Christian theology has always said that God's essence is unknowable. But we needn't despair, because God is known in and through the persons of God. We can know the persons of God. The God who is three persons in relationship enters into a relationship with us. So we're not praying to a 'thing', an 'it', a 'force' at all, nor to the transcendent Absolute of Western philosophy, nor the immanent force of Eastern religion. Who wants to pray to a thing? We don't relate to God in the same way as we relate to 'the government' or 'the idea of peace' or 'nature' or 'gravity'. The models we have are a child relating to his father, a sister to her brother, a wife to her husband, a friend to a friend.

2. Think about the one God

We pray conscious of the three persons. But we must never separate them, like tritheists – people who functionally believe in three gods. To encounter one divine person is to know the others. To see Jesus is to know the Father. The Spirit is the Spirit of Christ. This means we always have communion with God – not a part of God. If I have a communion with the Son, then I also have communion with the Father and the Spirit. If I am indwelt by the Spirit, then I am indwelt by the Son and the Father. If we forget the three are one, then we can start to think of Jesus as the nice version of God, with a nasty Father lurking in the background. But the Father is not a reluctant father who has to be won over by the Son. Our relationship of love with the triune God, which we express in prayer, was initiated by the Father. It is his eternal plan: 'For he chose us in him before the creation of the world to be holy and blameless in his sight. In love he predestined us for adoption to sonship through Jesus Christ, in accordance with his pleasure and will' (Ephesians 1:4–5). So it was the Father's plan to love us in Christ. He loves us as his children with the love he has for his own Son. The God we see in Christ is the real thing.

Psalm 84 begins:

> How lovely is your dwelling-place,
>   LORD Almighty!
> My soul yearns, even faints,
>   for the courts of the LORD;
> my heart and my flesh cry out
>   for the living God.
> (verses 1–2)

Sometimes I can become completely absorbed in a task. I once built some decking in our garden, and for two or three days it was all I could think about. I still had to eat and sleep. I still had meetings to attend. But all the time, I was eager to get back to building my decking. When I was tiling our kitchen, I couldn't sleep for thinking about tiling, so in the end I got up and worked through the night! Or think about someone who is newly in love. They still have to go to work and do the chores. But all the time, they're thinking about their loved one. In the same way, the more we see of the goodness and grace of God in Christ, the more our souls will yearn to be in his presence. Often I find prayer feels like a task I must complete before I get on with more interesting activities. But there have been times when this has been reversed, when I'm impatient with the routines of life because I want to get back to prayer. Or, better still, something of my enjoyment of God has suffused my day.

The rest of Psalm 84 describes how it's better to live in God's presence than anywhere else. Do you believe that? Sometimes I do, but most of the time, not really. What will make us change? The psalm ends:

> For the LORD God is a sun and shield;
>   the LORD bestows favour and honour;
> no good thing does he withhold
>   from those whose way of life is blameless.
> O LORD Almighty,
>   blessed is the one who trusts in you.
> (verses 11–12)

We will long to be in God's presence when we really believe the Lord is a sun and shield.

When you come before God in prayer, how do you imagine God? Do you imagine a boss checking your time sheet? Do you think of a schoolteacher correcting your mistakes? Or a king with better things to do? Or do you look into the eyes of a Father and see the sunshine of his love?

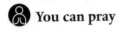 **You can pray**

A prayer based on Ephesians 3:16–21

> Our Father,
> we pray that out of your glorious riches
> you may strengthen us with power
> through your Spirit in our inner being,
> so that Christ may dwell in our hearts through faith.
>
> And we pray that we,
>   being rooted and established in love,

may have power,
   together with all your holy people,
to grasp how wide and long and high and deep
   is the love of Christ,
and to know this love that surpasses knowledge –
that we may be filled to the measure of all your fullness.

Now to you who is able to do
   immeasurably more than all we ask or imagine,
according to your power that is at work within us,
to you be glory in the church and in Christ Jesus
throughout all generations, for ever and ever! Amen.

5. 'I'VE GOT MORE URGENT THINGS TO DO'

Let me tell you what happens to me every morning. Around eight, I settle down to read my Bible and pray. In my mind, I've set aside an hour. Prayer, after all, is a key part of the work to which church leaders are to give themselves (Acts 6:3–4).

Except that at some point in that hour, I start to think about my work. I sit in a chair opposite my desk, so my computer is in front of me with a list of tasks for the day and emails to answer. I think to myself, 'I could get on with my work now.' But then I think, 'But prayer is important.' Backwards and forwards, I tussle in my mind. Eventually, I think, 'I know prayer's important, but I've prayed for everything on my list and I really want to get on with work.' And I get out of my armchair and go and sit at my desk. Every day, there's a point between eight and nine o'clock when I decide my work is more urgent than God's, that my contribution is more important than his, that I'll achieve more if I work than if I pray. Oh dear!

Prayer is nothing more and nothing less than a child asking her father for help. So why do I find it so hard? Because I don't desire intimacy with my Father or I don't feel the need of his help. Prayer becomes a tiresome duty instead of a joyful privilege. People in my prayer survey wrote,

- 'The hindrance to my prayers is self-reliance. I think I can sort it. It's often not until I'm really in a corner that I pray.'
- 'My pride hinders my prayer. I think I know what needs to happen or I trust in human activity.'

Why does God need our prayers to do his work? The answer is that he doesn't. But he *chooses* to work through our prayers. This raises the question of the link between our prayers and the sovereign will of God.

Why pray when God already knows what we need and has already decided what will happen? If God ordains all events as part of an eternal plan, what do we hope to achieve through prayer? If God is sovereign, why pray at all? Here's how people put it in my survey:

- 'My big question is: why pray? Since God is all-powerful and all-knowing, prayer seems somewhat superfluous. Yet I know it's vital because time and again I've seen it be effective.'
- 'How does someone who believes strongly in God's sovereignty find an urgency to pray more?'
- 'Does prayer actually change things, or is God just wanting to have a relationship with us?'
- 'The more I understand God as sovereign, the less I see prayer as "efficacious" and yet the more I pray. Now that I think about it, this is very paradoxical!'

- 'Why do we ask lots of people to pray about something if numbers don't affect the outcome?'
- 'How important and effective is quantity when it comes to prayer? Will the prayer warrior who stays up all night generate greater outcomes?'
- 'Even now, after being a Christian for three years, I often wonder whether prayer really makes a difference and what would happen if I didn't pray.'

Prayer changes the world
Some people answer these questions by saying that prayer only changes us – it doesn't change the world. As I pray for peace, I become a more peaceable person.

It's certainly true that prayer changes the pray-er, and this is a really important biblical point. Prayer involves bowing before the will of our heavenly Father. We pray with Christ, 'Your will be done' (Matthew 26:42). In Ephesians 1, Paul prays that believers 'may *know* [God] better . . . be *enlightened* in order that [they] may *know* the hope to which he has called [them] . . . and his incomparably great power' (verses 17–19, my italics). He's not praying for hope or power per se, but for a greater awareness of hope and power.

But internal change isn't the whole truth. Prayer really does change the world. God acts in response to our prayers. For example, he declares his intention to destroy the people of Israel, but refrains from doing so because of the prayers of Moses (Exodus 33:12–17; Numbers 14:11–20). James suggests there are things God doesn't do because we don't pray: 'You do not have because you do not ask God' (James 4:2). Although Paul prays for changed hearts in Ephesians 1, it's a change in the hearts of *other* people. Paul is not just opening himself up to change through prayer, but asking God to bring change in the world beyond himself.

The Bible even speaks of God himself changing in response to prayer. Amos saw God preparing locusts and fire in judgment, but, in response to Amos's prayer, 'the LORD relented' (Amos 7:1–6). This language involves an accommodation to our limited understanding. Elsewhere, the Bible says that God doesn't change his mind (Numbers 23:19; 1 Samuel 15:29). But even as we recognize the metaphorical nature of this language, we mustn't lose the force of the intended meaning: God really is open to the requests of his people. God responds to human activity – especially the prayers of his people (Jeremiah 18:8; 26:3, 13, 19; Joel 2:13–14; Jonah 3:10; 4:2). The Puritan Thomas Goodwin, in his book *The Return of Prayers*, encourages Christians to look for answers to prayer. He says, 'When a man hath put up prayers to God, he is to rest assured, that God will in mercy answer his prayers; and to listen diligently, and observe how his prayers are answered.'[1]

God controls the world

Others make sense of prayer by denying that God is sovereign or suggesting that his sovereignty is limited.[2] According to this view, prayer is given by God as an expression of human freedom in the sense that there are blessings God will only give if we pray. Or people say things like: 'God has been hindered in his purposes by our lack of willingness. When we learn his purposes and make them our prayers, we are giving him the opportunity to act.'[3] Such language suggests that prayer is about giving God permission to act.

God controls nature

The Bible, however, says that God is completely sovereign. He is sovereign over the natural world, controlling the weather (Psalms 65:9–11; 135:5–7; 147:15–18). 'I form the light and create darkness, I bring prosperity and create disaster; I, the

Lord, do all these things' (Isaiah 45:7; see also Genesis 41:32; Amos 3:6). He's intimately involved in the running of his world. Jesus says that every sparrow that falls and every hair on our heads is known and numbered by God (Luke 12:6–7). What appear to us as accidents happen because God allows them to happen (Exodus 21:13; 1 Kings 22:34). 'The lot is cast into the lap,' says Proverbs 16:33, 'but its every decision is from the Lord.'

God controls history

God is sovereign over human history. In Athens, Paul says, 'From one man he made all the nations, that they should inhabit the whole earth; and he marked out their appointed times in history and the boundaries of their lands' (Acts 17:26; see also Daniel 4:35). Psalm 33:10–11 says,

> The Lord foils the plans of the nations;
>> he thwarts the purposes of the peoples.
> But the plans of the Lord stand firm for ever,
>> the purposes of his heart through all generations.

(See also Psalms 115:2–3; 135:6; Proverbs 16:4.)

God controls people

God is also sovereign over the human heart. 'Many are the plans in a person's heart, but it is the Lord's purpose that prevails' (Proverbs 19:21). 'In the Lord's hand the king's heart is a stream of water that he channels towards all who please him' (Proverbs 21:1; see also Exodus 4:21; Joshua 11:20; 1 Kings 8:58; Psalm 105:25; Jeremiah 10:23).

In ways we can't fully understand, God weaves his sovereign purposes through the free decisions of human beings. Joseph was Jacob's favourite son born to his favourite wife. Jacob wasn't slow to express this, and Joseph wasn't slow to revel in it. So, in their jealousy, Joseph's brothers faked his death and sold him into slavery. It was a murky business all round! But God was working out his purposes. Joseph eventually became the prime minister of Egypt and used his position to save many people from famine, including the people of God from whom the promised Messiah would come. Joseph told his brothers, 'You intended to harm me, but God intended it for good to accomplish what is now being done, the saving of many lives' (Genesis 50:20).

The supreme example of this is the cross: at the cross God achieves his greatest purpose through the greatest sinful act of humanity. The early church prays, 'Herod and Pontius Pilate met together with the Gentiles and the people of Israel in this city to conspire against your holy servant Jesus, whom you anointed. They did what your power and will had decided beforehand should happen' (Acts 4:27–28). The cross is the ultimate act of evil, as humanity pushes God out of his world onto the cross. But even this evil act was part of God's sovereign plan 'for the saving of many lives'.

Our culture often sees human freedom as having a number of options open to us. The more options we have then the more free we are, according to this view. But if that's the nature of freedom, then I'm more free than God, because God can't choose to sin. Instead, the Bible sees freedom as the ability to do what we want or the ability to do what is right or, better still, the ability to be what we are intended to be. So God is the *most* free being because he can do whatever he wants and he always does what is right. Joseph's brothers were free to do what they wanted to do. So were Herod and Pilate. But their free choices conformed to God's purpose to save many people. They weren't free to act contrary to God's purpose, but they were free to do what they wanted.

There are many prayers – such as the request that a par-ticular person might be converted – that make no sense if God is *not* sovereign over human hearts. In Romans 9:15, Paul quotes Exodus 33:19 where God says, 'I will have mercy on whom I have mercy, and I will have compassion on whom I have compassion.' A few verses later, Paul says, 'My heart's desire and prayer to God for the Israelites is that they may be saved' (Romans 10:1). Paul prays for the conversion of his fellow Jews, because it's God who sovereignly shows mercy on whom he chooses to show mercy. The quote from Exodus 33 comes as God reveals himself to Moses after the Israelites have built a golden calf. God had told Moses that he was going to destroy his people. But Moses interceded and 'then the LORD relented and did not bring on his people the disaster he had threatened' (Exodus 32:14). God is sovereign in mercy and judgment. And because he's sovereign, Moses and Paul pray.

Again in Romans 9, Paul describes God as a potter working the clay of humanity, shaping us according to his design. And we have no more right to challenge his will than a lump of clay can speak back to the potter: 'Does not the potter have the right to make out of the same lump of clay some pottery for special purposes and some for common use?' (Romans 9:21). This is an allusion to Jeremiah's visit to a potter: 'The pot he was shaping from the clay was marred in his hands; so the potter formed it into another pot, shaping it as seemed best to him' (Jeremiah 18:4). The message is clear. God has a right to shape as he chooses. But notice how God applies this message:

> Then the word of the LORD came to me. He said, 'Can I not do with you, Israel, as this potter does?' declares the LORD. 'Like clay in the hand of the potter, so are you in my hand, Israel. If at any time I announce that a nation or kingdom is to be uprooted, torn

down and destroyed, and if that nation I warned repents of its evil, then I will relent and not inflict on it the disaster I had planned. And if at another time I announce that a nation or kingdom is to be built up and planted, and if it does evil in my sight and does not obey me, then I will reconsider the good I had intended to do for it.'
(Jeremiah 18:5–10)

God's sovereignty includes his right to respond to the actions (including the prayers) of people and 'reconsider' what he had previously announced would happen.

We best express our belief in God's sovereignty when we pray with the expectation that God can intervene in human lives and human history to bring about the things for which we pray. This God to whom we pray can '[work] out everything in conformity with the purpose of his will' so that our prayers can be effective (Ephesians 1:11). Instead of thinking of the sovereignty of God as something which impedes prayer, we should think of it as the space in which prayer is effective.

The power of prayer and the control of God
The Bible, then, assures us both that God changes the world in response to prayer and that God is eternally sovereign. God's sovereignty doesn't compromise our responsibility to pray. And we're responsible to pray, but not in a way that compromises God's sovereignty.

Beyond these affirmations, we need to be cautious. We can't fully understand the mechanics of God's sovereignty. But we can say that the claim that God changes reality in response to prayer is not incompatible with his sovereignty, because God's response to our prayers is itself part of his sovereign plan.

Why did it rain yesterday? You could say that God chose that it would rain. Or you could describe the water cycle: it rained because clouds formed in the sky. Which is true? Is rain caused by God or by clouds? The answer, of course, is both. It's a false choice. Both can be true at the same time. God chose that it would rain. But he chose to cause rain by sending clouds (as he normally does). He ordained the effect (rain) and also the cause (clouds).

It's the same with prayer. Why did God heal my friend yesterday? You could answer that it had always been God's plan to heal him. Or you could say he was healed as a result of my prayers. Both are true. God ordained the healing of my friend. But as part of that eternal plan, he also chose to heal him in response to my prayers. My prayers were as much part of that plan as the healing itself. So we can say that my friend would not have been healed if I hadn't prayed. God planned the effect (the healing) and the cause (my prayers). Of course, my prayers might not be the only cause. Other people may also have prayed. A trip to the doctor's may have been another cause. But it could be that in God's plan my prayers were a necessary cause.

George Müller, the nineteenth-century evangelist famous for his orphanage in Bristol, once decided to pray for the conversion of five friends. After a few months, one of them came to Christ. It was another ten years before two more were saved. Müller continued praying for the final two. He was once asked whether he really thought God would save them. 'Do you think God would have kept me praying for them all these years if he did not intend to save them?' he answered.[4] One was saved after twenty-five years of prayer, and Müller kept praying for the final friend for fifty-two years until his death. His friend was converted shortly after Müller's funeral. God prompts us to pray so he can answer and bring about his will through our prayers.

So our prayers are not a limit to God's sovereignty, but the ultimate expression of it. God is able to achieve his will in response to our prayers. The theologian P. T. Forsyth put it like this:

> If our prayers reach or move Him it is because He first reached and moved us to pray . . . The world was made by a freedom which not only left room for the kindred freedom of prayer, but which so ordered all things in its own interest that in their deepest depths they conspire to produce prayer . . . Our prayer is more than the acceptance by us of God's will; it is its assertion in us . . . Prayer is that will of God's making itself good . . . So when God yields to prayer in the name of Christ, to the prayer of faith and love, He yields to Himself who inspired it.[5]

God wants us to pray because he wants a relationship with us. In Gethsemane, Jesus asked for the cup of suffering to be taken away. So he prayed a prayer he knew was contrary to God's will! That's why he goes on to say, 'Yet not what I will, but what you will' (Mark 14:36). Asking for what he knew to be contrary to God's will makes no sense if you view prayer as a slot machine for gaining divine favours. But it makes perfect sense for Jesus to talk about his horror at what he was about to face when you see prayer as the expression of a relationship.

If you pray, then God has chosen to accomplish his purposes with your participation. If you don't pray, then God has chosen to accomplish his purposes without your participation. So your lack of prayer doesn't thwart his purposes. He can just as well do it without your participation as with your participation. He can do it through your prayers or he can do it without your prayers.

This is liberating. It means you don't have to cover all the bases for your family and friends to be safe. The fruitfulness of your church, the safety of your family, the needs of the oppressed don't depend on your praying 'enough'.

But it's also motivating. Who loses out if you don't pray? You do! When you pray, you're given the privilege of participating in God's purposes. God wants your cooperation. Paul writes, 'On him we have set our hope that he will continue to deliver us, as you help us by your prayers' (2 Corinthians 1:10–11). What he says literally is: 'as you cooperate on our behalf'. In prayer, you cooperate with God in his great plans of deliverance.

This means you can't manipulate God in prayer. You can't twist his arm by praying for a long time – God is sovereign. Yet God sovereignly chooses to use your passionate, persistent prayers as an appointed means by which things happen.

I pray because prayer changes things. That's actually shorthand for: 'God changes things in response to prayer.' But it's a perfectly serviceable shorthand. God ordains that my prayers change things. This means I can legitimately say, 'This happened because I prayed.'

It might be that we don't see more of God's blessing because we don't pray. If God did bless our prayer-less work, then we might think it was our achievement and not his. If we worked without ever needing to pray, then we might assume it was our work that counted. But we have to pray so that we're constantly reminded that it's God's work and God's glory.

Reflection

- 'Why pray when God already knows what we need and has already decided what will happen?'
- 'How does someone who believes strongly in God's sovereignty find an urgency to pray more?'

- 'Does prayer actually change things, or is God just wanting to have a relationship with us?'
- 'Why do we ask lots of people to pray about something if numbers don't affect the outcome?'

How would you answer these questions?

Praying as if God matters

We find it hard to pray because, in our heart of hearts, at the start of a busy day, when we see our inboxes and the problems we face, we don't really believe that 'power belongs to you, God' (Psalm 62:11). We overestimate what we can do and underestimate what God can do. Suppose, for example, you're a parent struggling to discipline a child. We assume it's within our power to solve the problem and end up saying things like: 'Why do I have to tell you so many times?' Perhaps the answer to that question is that we've been too self-reliant to pray. Paul Miller writes,

> We tell ourselves, 'Strong Christians pray a lot. If I were a stronger Christian, I'd pray more.' Strong Christians do pray more, but they pray more because they realize how weak they are. They don't try to hide it from themselves. Weakness is the channel that allows them to access grace . . . We don't need self-discipline to pray continuously; we just need to be poor in spirit. Poverty of spirit makes room for his Spirit. It creates a God-shaped hole in our hearts and offers us a new way to relate to others.[6]

Why do we find it hard to pray? We think too much depends on *us*. If we believed everything depended on God, then we would pour out our hearts to him. No-one would be able to shut us up. I'm not worried about how long you pray. God doesn't measure the worth of our prayers with a stopwatch, but by the blood of his precious Son. The issue is not whether you get up early or pray through the night. But we should pray as if it's God's work that matters, not ours. That's my problem each morning when I think that what I do counts more than what God does.

I was recently involved in pastoring a couple who had been married for nearly fifteen years. Their relationship had almost completely broken down. As I talked with them, they each blamed the other and often couldn't even agree on the bare facts. Over several months, I met with them without seeing any progress. They were despairing. I was despairing. I found it impossible to disentangle what was happening, let alone discern any way forward. In the end, I simply called them to read the Bible with me and pray together in response. Three or four weeks later, the husband rang. 'Something's changed,' he said. 'Things are much better.' 'What happened?' I asked. 'What's made the difference?' 'I don't know,' he replied, 'but it started when we prayed together.' Of course, I had prayed for them from the beginning. But there came a point when prayer felt like the only option left. Perhaps we only really pray when we realize we can't change the world. In desperation, we turn to God in prayer and find that God changes the world in response to our prayers.

A bricklayer was swearing in front of the home of the Victorian preacher, Charles Spurgeon. So Spurgeon offered him £100 if he would never use the name of God again. The man readily pocketed the money. But when he got home, he found his daughter was sick. For three nights, she was ill. But the man couldn't call on God's name. Eventually, he went to Spurgeon and threw his money back at him saying, 'Prayer is worth more than all the money in the world.' What's prayer worth to you?

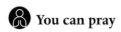 You can pray

A prayer based on Ephesians 1:17–19

O Lord, the God of our Lord Jesus Christ,
our glorious Father,
may you give us the Spirit of wisdom and revelation,
so that we may know you better.
We pray that the eyes of our hearts may be enlightened
in order that we may know the hope to which you have called us,
the riches of your glorious inheritance in your holy people,
and your incomparably great power for us who believe. Amen.

6. 'WHEN I NEEDED HIM, GOD DIDN'T ANSWER'

'Why are so many prayers seemingly not answered?' asked someone in my survey. For some, this is a fascinating intellectual question. But for many, it is deeply personal and extremely painful. You may have prayed for the conversion of a loved one, and he or she has not been converted. You may have prayed for healing and not been healed. Your life may have fallen apart, and it's felt as if God has been indifferent to your pleas for mercy.

This was the experience of the writer of Lamentations. 'You have covered yourself with a cloud so that no prayer can get through,' he says in Lamentations 3:44. It's a powerful image. People sometimes pull their clothing over their heads when they don't want to talk. For the writer of Lamentations, it feels as if God is doing this, but God has wrapped a cloud around himself 'so that no prayer can get through'.

The writer of Lamentations is not alone. Here's a selection of comments and questions from my survey:

- 'Why, after forty years of praying, does my mother have no interest in Christ?'
- 'Why don't I see more positive answers to my prayers?'
- 'How can I pray when I feel the Lord is disciplining me?'
- 'Why, after two years of fervent prayer for my daughter's marriage, does her husband continue to walk away from her and redefine his faith to justify it?'
- 'Why does God choose not to intervene when we've prayed something specific and obviously good?'

We don't know for sure who wrote the book of Lamentations (though it may have been the prophet Jeremiah). But we do know it was written after the fall of Jerusalem. In the sixth century BC, Jeremiah and others warned God's people to turn from their idolatry and injustice. But they didn't listen, and God's judgment came in the form of the Babylonian army. The Babylonians defeated Judah, deposed the king, deported the people and destroyed the temple in 587 BC. The book of Lamentations is a lament for this event. The writer's world has completely collapsed, and God seems far away.

The temple was decorated with palm trees and pomegranates as a deliberate echo of Eden. It was a symbolic recreation of the garden where God had walked with humanity. This would be the place where people could meet God. When the temple was finished, the ark of the covenant, the symbol of God's presence and the place of atonement, was brought to the new temple in great procession with the people singing, 'He is good; his love endures for ever' (2 Chronicles 5:13). When the ark arrived we read: 'Then the temple of the LORD was filled with the cloud, and the priests could not perform their service because of the cloud, for the glory of the LORD filled the temple of God' (2 Chronicles 5:13–14). The living

God had come to dwell among his people. Then Solomon prays a wonderful prayer:

> May your eyes be open towards this temple day and night, this place of which you said you would put your Name there. May you hear the prayer your servant prays towards this place. Hear the supplications of your servant and of your people Israel when they pray towards this place. Hear from heaven, your dwelling-place; and when you hear, forgive.
>
> (2 Chronicles 6:20–21)

God comes to Solomon after the inauguration of the temple and reiterates his promise that he will hear when people pray towards the temple: 'My eyes will be open and my ears attentive to the prayers offered in this place . . . My eyes and my heart will always be there' (2 Chronicles 7:12–16). It's a beautiful promise.

But now the temple is destroyed. God no longer dwells in his temple. He has abandoned his people. When they turn in prayer towards the temple, they see only rubble. The temple, the great symbol of God's presence, has become a symbol of his absence.

Lamentations is a heartfelt, pain-ridden cry of anguish from someone who is experiencing personal tragedy, communal tragedy and spiritual tragedy. Much of it is unrelenting. At the literary and theological centre of Lamentations in chapter 3 is hope for everyone who feels abandoned by God. But even this is set in the context of an expression of God's abandonment. 'He has driven me away and made me walk in darkness rather than light' (3:2); 'He has made me dwell in darkness like those long dead' (3:6); 'My eyes will flow unceasingly, without relief, until the LORD looks down from heaven and sees' (3:49–50). Perhaps you can echo these sentiments. You feel that God doesn't hear your prayers. When you've needed him most, God hasn't been there for you. Perhaps verse 8 describes your experience: 'Even when I call out or cry for help, he shuts out my prayer.'

1. Examine your heart and repent of your sin

When relationships break down it's often because one party has stopped communicating. And it may be that you feel far from God because you've stopped talking to him. Or you've distanced yourself from God through your sin. You may be the one who's hiding – just like Adam and Eve in the Garden of Eden. So the writer gives us an invitation:

> Let us examine our ways and test them,
> and let us return to the LORD.
> Let us lift up our hearts and our hands
> to God in heaven, and say:
> 'We have sinned and rebelled
> and you have not forgiven.'
> (Lamentations 3:40–42)

Don't misunderstand this point. Sin is not always the reason for unanswered prayer. In fact, in John 9, Jesus meets a man who has been blind from birth, and his disciples ask whether he's blind because of his sin or his parents' sin. '"Neither this man nor his parents sinned," said Jesus, "but this happened so that the works of God might be displayed in him"' (John 9:3). As we shall see, your prayers may be unanswered so that the works of God might be displayed in your life. It may not be because you've sinned. But on the other hand, it might be.

'Let us examine our ways . . . let us return to the LORD' is a gracious invitation to turn back to God, to reconnect. God cannot and will not punish his people, because at the cross Christ has already born the penalty of our sin in full. And God will not punish us, because 'his compassions never fail' (Lamentations 3:22). So he is not punishing you. But he may be inviting you to 'return' to him (3:40), to acknowledge that you've sinned and receive his forgiveness.

It was more complicated for Israel. The nation was a mixed community with believers and unbelievers. The Babylonian army was an instrument of God's judgment against unbelieving Israel. Problems in the life of an unbeliever are a gracious call to repent before it's too late, a kind of hell-in-miniature to warn people what's coming. Romans 1 talks about 'the wrath of God . . . being revealed' as God gives us over to our sin (1:18, 24, 26, 28).

If you're a Christian, then God is not punishing you. But unanswered prayer may be his discipline, a call to turn back from sin to God.

At this point, it's helpful to consider the circumstances in which the Bible says God will *not* hear and answer our prayers.

It's really important as we explore this to distinguish between God refusing to hear our prayers and God answering our prayers in ways that are different from our requests. God always answers our prayers in his wisdom, for our good and for his glory. So it might be the case that you've prayed with a pure heart in the name of Jesus. It may well even be a legitimate request. But God may not give what you ask, because what you've asked is not wise or not for your good or not for his glory, and so not in accordance with his will. But God still hears these prayers and in a sense still answers them by giving us that for which we should have asked – what is ultimately for our good and his glory. Think of a child who asks her father for chocolate and is given fruit. The fruit is an answer to her request, albeit not the specific answer for which she was looking. And it's an answer that's for her good. She might even come to recognize this next time she visits the dentist! This gives us a great freedom in prayer. We don't have to work out the precise request we need to make – we can trust God to answer in his wisdom and love.

But the Bible does describe certain circumstances in which God refuses to listen to our prayers. God will not hear us when:

1. *We harbour sin in our hearts against God.* 'If I had cherished sin in my heart, the Lord would not have listened' (Psalm 66:18; see also Ezekiel 14:1–5).
2. *We harbour sin in our hearts against other people.*

> When you spread out your hands in prayer,
>   I hide my eyes from you;
> even when you are offering many prayers,
>   I am not listening.
> Your hands are full of blood! . . .
> Learn to do right; seek justice.
>   Defend the oppressed.
> Take up the cause of the fatherless,
>   plead the case of the widow.
> (Isaiah 1:15, 17; see also Isaiah 58)

'Husbands . . . be considerate as you live with your wives, and treat them with respect as the weaker partner and as heirs with you of the gracious gift of life, so that nothing will hinder your prayers' (1 Peter 3:7).

3. *We pray to impress other people.* 'When you pray, do not be like the hypocrites, for they love to pray standing in the synagogues and on the street corners to be seen by others. Truly I tell you, they have received their reward in full' (Matthew 6:5).

4. *We make selfish requests.* 'Their mouths speak of love, but their hearts are greedy for unjust gain' (Ezekiel 33:31). 'When you ask, you do not receive, because you ask with wrong motives, that you may spend what you get on your pleasures' (James 4:3).

What the above have in common is a lack of sincerity. In each case, the person we present in prayer is not our real selves. Rather it's a godly version of ourselves, when in fact we're cherishing sin or pride or selfishness. Such prayers don't come from the heart. In Isaiah 29:13, God says, 'These people come near to me with their mouth and honour me with their lips, but their hearts are far from me.' Charles Spurgeon says,

> God looks not at the elegancy of your prayers, to see how neat they are;
> nor yet at the geometry of your prayers, to see how long they are;
> nor yet at the arithmetic of your prayers, to see how many they are;
> nor yet at the music of your prayers,
> nor yet at the sweetness of your voice,
> nor yet at the logic of your prayers;
> but at the sincerity of your prayers, how hearty they are.[1]

If we sin, then we have a thousand Scripture promises to help us come before God to find mercy. Sin is no obstacle to prayer, because God welcomes repentant sinners! But if we *harbour* sin in our hearts, whether against God or others, then we won't want to pray. Or if we do, we will be hypocrites, hiding our sin and pretending we don't need mercy. God doesn't require us to be perfect before we can pray, but he does expect us to be honest. That's because prayer is the expression of a relationship. It's a relationship of grace, but it's still a relationship.

I know in my own experience that if I'm refusing to say 'no' to temptation or holding on to a sinful attitude, then I can't pray. I can't come before God in prayer and pretend everything is OK. So, if I am nurturing sin in my heart, I need to repudiate that sin as I start praying. And sometimes, I don't want to do that. So the price I pay for nurturing sin is not being able to pray. But that is too high a price. The thought of a day without prayer is too much to contemplate.

One morning recently, for example, there was bitterness in my heart. Then, when I walked out of my door, it was such a beautiful day that my heart was lifted in praise. I felt compelled to thank God. But that meant I first had to repudiate my sin. I couldn't pray while I harboured sin in my heart. The only solution was repentance.

The really important thing to realize is that it's *not God* who's holding us at arm's length. *We're* holding God at arm's length. That's why he feels distant – because we're either pushing him away (by harbouring sin in our hearts) or hiding behind a mask. If God feels far away, then examine your life. If you're living with unrepentant sin, then God will feel far away because you're holding him at a distance.

But the great news is that God is always ready to receive us back. None of these things represents any reluctance or hesitation on his part. He's like the father of the prodigal son, ready to run to embrace you. So ask the Holy Spirit to examine you, show you the sinful desires in your life and convict you of sin. Pray with the psalmist,

Search me, God, and know my heart;
    test me and know my anxious thoughts.
See if there is any offensive way in me,
    and lead me in the way everlasting.
(Psalm 139:23–24)

2. Wait for the coming of God

It may be that you examine yourself and don't discover a sin of which you need to repent. Of course, none of us is without sin. But there may be no persistent sin keeping you from God. Or you may be aware of sin, but also be repentant and committed to change. Like Job, there may be nothing to which you can point.

What should we do in such cases? Lamentations 3:24–30 says,

> I say to myself, 'The LORD is my portion;
>   therefore I will wait for him.'
>
> The LORD is good to those whose hope is in him,
>   to the one who seeks him;
> it is good to wait quietly
>   for the salvation of the LORD.
> It is good for a man to bear the yoke
>   while he is young.
>
> Let him sit alone in silence,
>   for the LORD has laid it on him.
> Let him bury his face in the dust –
>   there may yet be hope.
> Let him offer his cheek to one who would strike him,
>   and let him be filled with disgrace.

Notice the word 'hope' (in verses 21, 25 and 29), and notice the word 'wait' (in verses 24 and 26). 'I say to myself, "The LORD is my portion; therefore I will wait for him."' 'It is good to wait quietly for the salvation of the LORD.' The Bible often invites us to wait for God. Genesis 49:18; Psalms 25:3–5, 21; 37:9, 34; 39:7; 52:9; 69:6; Isaiah 8:17; 26:8–11; 33:2;

Hosea 12:6; Romans 8:23–25; 1 Corinthians 1:7; Galatians 5:5; 1 Thessalonians 1:10 all talk about 'waiting' for God (though the word is sometimes translated 'looking' or 'hoping').

> Wait for the LORD;
>> be strong and take heart
>> and wait for the LORD.
> (Psalm 27:14)

> I wait for the LORD, my whole being waits,
>> and in his word I put my hope.
> I wait for the Lord
>> more than watchmen wait for the morning,
>> more than watchmen wait for the morning.
> (Psalm 130:5–6)

We want God to act, to come, to speak. And God says, 'Wait.' This involves an attitude of patience – not telling God how he should act. But it's also an attitude of faith and expectation – not giving up on God.

Waiting is very counter-cultural. We don't like waiting. We complain if we have to queue for a few minutes or wait a few seconds for a webpage to open. And we want a religion to match. We want a solution that can be applied to every problem with immediate results. But God is not working on our timescales. He has all the time in the world. He's like a sculptor shaping you as a person. And he's a creating a master-piece because he's shaping you into the image of his Son. But he's not working with inanimate stone. No, he is working with a human soul. And his tools are not a hammer and chisel, but the circumstances of your life. You can't hurry him up as he pursues that task.[2] Sometimes he wants us to wait, to be patient, to let him do his work. And we can wait in hope because God will come:

> For no one is cast off
>   by the Lord for ever.
> Though he brings grief, he will show compassion,
>   so great is his unfailing love.
> For he does not willingly bring affliction
>   or grief to anyone.
>
> To crush underfoot
>   all prisoners in the land,
> to deny people their rights
>   before the Most High,
> to deprive them of justice –
>   would not the Lord see such things?
> (Lamentations 3:31–36)

God sees your affliction. He sees injustice. And he will act. This is the very centre of the book of Lamentations. God will indeed come to those who wait for him (Psalm 40:1–3; Isaiah 25:9; 40:29–31; 49:22–23).

Often God comes in this life. Perhaps your prayers will be answered. You may have a clear experience of God or a new or a renewed confidence in his love. I think of friends who've longed for a child and eventually, after many years and much heartbreak, have conceived. But I also think of other friends who've had to come to terms with being childless, yet have discovered a richness in Christ that enables them to be content in him.

God doesn't always bring joy in this life. Some people are martyred for Christ without divine intervention. Many endure suffering throughout their lives. But 'no one is cast off by the

Lord for ever' (verse 31). God will come, if not in this life, then in the next one. Stephen, the first Christian martyr, died without God acting to prevent his death. But as he died, he saw a vision of heaven open to welcome him into the presence of Jesus. In 1555, the English Reformers, Hugh Latimer and Nicholas Ridley, were burnt at the stake for their gospel convictions. But they died confident that their martyrdom was part of God's purpose. As the flames rose, Latimer famously said, 'Be of good cheer, Master Ridley, and play the man, for we shall this day light such a candle in England as I trust by God's grace shall never be put out.'

Nobody is ever God's debtor. Whatever has happened or not happened in this life, none of us will stand in the new creation and feel we've been short-changed by God. In the New Testament, waiting is commonly directed towards the return of Christ and the renewal of all things:

- 'We wait eagerly for our adoption to sonship, the redemption of our bodies' (Romans 8:23).
- '[We] eagerly wait for our Lord Jesus Christ to be revealed' (1 Corinthians 1:7).
- 'For through the Spirit we eagerly await by faith the righteousness for which we hope' (Galatians 5:5).
- 'And [we] wait for [God's] Son from heaven, whom he raised from the dead – Jesus, who rescues us from the coming wrath' (1 Thessalonians 1:10).

In Revelation, we read: 'The four living creatures and the twenty-four elders fell down before the Lamb. Each one had a harp and they were holding golden bowls full of incense, which are the prayers of God's people' (5:8). This is the court of heaven. And the prayers of the saints are symbolized by bowls of incense. Just as the smell of incense rises into the nostrils, so our prayers come before God. There before the throne of God are *your* prayers. Then, in Revelation 8:3–5, we read:

> Another angel, who had a golden censer, came and stood at the altar. He was given much incense to offer, with the prayers of all God's people, on the golden altar in front of the throne. The smoke of the incense, together with the prayers of God's people, went up before God from the angel's hand. Then the angel took the censer, filled it with fire from the altar, and hurled it on the earth; and there came peals of thunder, rumblings, flashes of lightning and an earthquake.

It's as if our prayers have been stored up in the bowls and are now offered up to God. As a result, fire from the altar is hurled to the earth and the seven trumpets are unleashed. These represent God's purposes in history which come to a climax in the return of Christ and the final judgment.

It may be that your unanswered prayers are in one of those bowls even as we speak. God is waiting until the time is right. And one day, your prayers will unleash the renewal of all things. When you pray for justice, the ultimate answer may be the final judgment. When you pray for peace, the ultimate answer may be the reign of the Lamb. When you pray for health, the ultimate answer may be your resurrection body. When you pray for joy, the ultimate answer may be the wedding feast of the Lamb. And when you pray for a sense of God's presence, the ultimate answer may be the day heaven comes to earth and 'a loud voice from the throne' says, 'Look! God's dwelling-place is now among the people, and he will dwell with them. They will be his people, and God himself will be with them and be their God' (Revelation 21:3).

3. Trust in the providence of God

Sometimes God has another agenda altogether. Our priorities are not always his priorities. We can think God is doing nothing because we're looking in the wrong place. What looks to us like unanswered prayer may be prayer God is answering in a different but better way:

> Though he brings grief, he will show compassion,
> so great is his unfailing love.
> For he does not willingly bring affliction
> or grief to anyone.
> (Lamentations 3:32–33)

God brings grief, but not willingly. He does it to achieve a bigger purpose which is that we might have joy in him. Verse 38 says, 'Is it not from the mouth of the Most High that both calamities and good things come?' Both good and evil are part of God's sovereign plan. But 'God does not stand behind good and evil in exactly the same way'.[3] He allows evil and uses it for his good purposes, but he's not the source of evil in the way that's he's the source of all that is good. He sends good things because they are good. He sends evil things to achieve good. 'Though he brings grief, he will show compassion, *so great is his unfailing love*' (verse 32, my italics). There's a sense

---

Reflection

- What do we learn in Hebrews 12:4–11 about God's discipline?
- How does this match your experience?
- What's the difference between discipline and punishment?

in which, even when God grieves you for the sake of his bigger purposes, he's longing to show compassion because his love is so great. It's full to bursting.

We mustn't think of God's discipline as God correcting us whenever we do something wrong – like a slap on the wrist. It's bigger and broader than that. It's God's training regime to shape us into the image of Christ. God may not answer your prayers in order to humble your pride or teach you empathy with others. Or so that you long for him all the more. There may be something you desire that God is not giving: a spouse, healing, work, success in ministry. It might well be a good thing. But, while you want this, God wants you. He wants your love. He wants you to desire him above everything else. As Matt Chandler says, 'God wounds like a surgeon.'[4] He cuts out from our lives whatever would destroy or weaken us. Earthly fathers can sometimes be nagged into giving us what we want. That's because sometimes they say 'no' because they can't be bothered. So nagging eventually succeeds because the bother of saying 'no' becomes more than the bother of saying 'yes'! But when God says 'no', it's never because he can't be bothered, but because his way really is best.

Gerv Markham is a husband and father in our church. In 2000, a couple of months after he became a Christian, he found a lump in his neck. Nine months later, he was finally diagnosed with a rare form of cancer. It's led to multiple operations as the cancer continues to appear in different parts of his body. Altogether, these surgical procedures have resulted in over three and a half feet of scars. Sooner or later, the cancer will catch up with him again, and his prognosis is very uncertain. Despite all this, Gerv says, 'My cancer was designed for me by God for his good purposes.' He acknowledges that some Christians get to see what God's purposes for their suffering are, while for others it remains a mystery. 'It's been a great blessing for me,' he says, 'to look back on what's happened to me and clearly see God working.'

> I have a much stronger hope of heaven, a much greater desire to live each day for him and to use every moment for his glory and to advance the gospel. And I've also had great opportunities to talk to people about what God has done in my life and how he's used this to bring me to greater godliness and turn me more into the person I was destined to be and that he wants me to be. And so I look at those things and I think, 'How could he not have done that when it's had such good effects?'[5]

One of our problems is that we remember unanswered prayer because the need remains. But we too often quickly forget answered prayer because the need has now gone away! So make sure you thank God for what he *is* doing in your life. You might want to record your prayer requests in a journal to help identify God's answers. Paul's remedy for worry is: 'Do not be anxious about anything, but in every situation, by prayer and petition, with thanksgiving, present your requests to God' (Philippians 4:6). We hand over, as it were, our problems to God. But notice, too, the words 'with thanksgiving'. Thanksgiving gives us perspective. We tend to focus on what God has not done and miss all that he has actually done. Paul goes on: 'Whatever is true, whatever is noble, whatever is right, whatever is pure, whatever is lovely, whatever is admirable – if anything is excellent or praiseworthy – think about such things' (Philippians 4:8).

4. Look at the character of God
The book of Lamentations begins and ends with the absence of God. But at its centre, there's a wonderful affirmation of God's compassion:

I remember my affliction and my wandering,
　　the bitterness and the gall.
I well remember them,
　　and my soul is downcast within me.
Yet this I call to mind
　　and therefore I have hope . . .
(Lamentations 3:19–21)

Before we come to God's compassion, notice that there's no hope to be found in living in denial. 'I remember my affliction,' the writer says. Hope is not found in denying or minimizing these circumstances. When he thinks about Jerusalem, his soul is downcast (verse 20). Hope is not found in denying what is true. Instead, hope is found is affirming what is *also* true. It's true that he's afflicted. But that's not the only thing that's true. The truth that brings hope is the truth about God:

Yet this I call to mind
　　and therefore I have hope:

Because of the LORD's great love we are not consumed,
　　for his compassions never fail.
They are new every morning;
　　great is your faithfulness.
I say to myself, 'The LORD is my portion;
　　therefore I will wait for him.'
(Lamentations 3:21–24)

Verse 38 says, 'Is it not from the mouth of the Most High that both calamities and good things come?' That God sends the calamities in our lives is a mystery, but it's also a comfort. Consider the alternatives. What if calamities were the result of blind fate? Or the outcome of our folly? Or ultimately rooted in demonic activity? Then we would truly have reason to fear. But, while our folly or demonic activity may be the immediate cause of problems, the ultimate source is God, for he's sovereign over all things. And this is good news because it means the One from whom calamities come is the One whose love is great. The struggles in your marriage, your unemployment, your cancer, your bereavement come from the One whose compassions never fail. Hope is found in the character of God. Our experience of him can fluctuate. Sometimes he feels near, sometimes far away. But his character is constant; he's unchanging.

God's ways may be a mystery, but his character is clear. Deuteronomy 29:29 says, 'The secret things belong to the LORD our God, but the things revealed belong to us and to our children for ever, that we may follow all the words of this law.' In other words, we don't know the mysteries of God's will. We can't always know why he chooses to work as he does: why in one situation he sends bad things and in another good things. I can't tell you why God hasn't answered your prayers in the way you want. These are the secret things of the Lord. But he has revealed himself. And what God has revealed *is* for us to know. And he has revealed himself as a good God, full of love, a God of compassion and unfailing faithfulness.

The poet William Cowper, a close friend and neighbour of John Newton in Olney, Buckinghamshire, suffered much from depression and doubt. At times, he was suicidal. Despite his doubts, Cowper could write in the hymn 'God Moves in a Mysterious Way':

> Deep in unfathomable mines
> of never failing skill
> he treasures up his bright designs
> and works his sovereign will.

Judge not the Lord by feeble sense,
but trust him for his grace;
behind a frowning providence
he hides a smiling face.

His purposes will ripen fast,
unfolding every hour;
the bud may have a bitter taste,
but sweet will be the flower.

The great demonstration of God's character is the cross. One of the striking things about Lamentations 3 is that, though it's a lament for the defeat of Jerusalem, it's also very personal. This is the voice of an individual, not a people. Moreover, though God doesn't punish his people, this person has experienced God's judgment. It begins, 'I am the man who has seen affliction by the rod of the LORD's wrath.' What's going on? The ultimate destruction of God's people came at the cross. Jesus our representative died in our place. At his trial, Jesus was struck round the head, an echo of verse 30 which says, 'Let him offer his cheek to one who would strike him.' God's judgment doesn't fall on his people because it has fallen on his Son.

At the cross, we see the love of God written large:

- 'God demonstrates his own love for us in this: while we were still sinners, Christ died for us' (Romans 5:8).
- 'This is love: not that we loved God, but that he loved us and sent his Son as an atoning sacrifice for our sins' (1 John 4:10).
- 'He who did not spare his own Son, but gave him up for us all – how will he not also, along with him, graciously give us all things?' (Romans 8:32).

Trouble, hardship, persecution, famine, nakedness, danger and sword are, says Paul, all a normal part of the Christian life. But they cannot separate us from Christ's love (Romans 8:17, 35–39).

In the midst of your turmoil, when you remember your affliction, when your soul is downcast, call this to mind: 'Because of the LORD's great love we are not consumed, for his compassions never fail' (3:22). Look through the gloom and see the cross. Lamentations 3:37–39 says,

> Who can speak and have it happen
>   if the Lord has not decreed it?
> Is it not from the mouth of the Most High
>   that both calamities and good things come?
> Why should the living complain
>   when punished for their sins?

In other words, God is sovereign and we have no leverage over him. Indeed, if God *were* punishing us, we couldn't complain. But this we know: in his love, the Father sent his Son to bear the punishment we deserve.

God the Father is *always* kind to us. He cannot and will not punish those who are in Christ. He always treats us with the love that he has towards his own Son. So whenever you turn towards him, he is ready to listen and willing to bless. He *always* regards us with affection, is *always* ready to hear our prayers. If he disciplines, it's always for our good. You may not understand what God is doing or why. But this you can know: 'God so loved the world that he gave his one and only Son, that whoever believes in him shall not perish but have eternal life' (John 3:16).

In Lamentations 3:24 the writer says to himself, 'The LORD is my portion; therefore I will wait for him.' When I was a child, I remember fighting with my sisters over pudding portions. We were always checking who had the largest helping. And if it wasn't us, then we felt disgruntled. In a way, that's an image for all of life. We're always looking at other people to see whether their 'portion' is bigger or better. The portion to which verse 24 alludes is probably a person's inheritance in the Promised Land. In an agrarian economy, land was the main measure of success. But now the land is under enemy occupation, and the people have been stripped of their 'portion' through exile.

What's on your plate at the moment? What's your portion? How does it compare to others? However we answer those questions and whatever the problems we face, we can say this: 'The LORD is my portion.'

In December 2010, Matthew Knell was diagnosed with leukaemia at the age of nineteen. He died a year later. A few weeks before his death, he sent a letter to his former colleagues at the outdoor activity centre where he'd been working. In it he wrote,

> Being in the hospital . . . I was suddenly faced with the reality
> of death . . . I've learnt . . . what's important and what's not.
> 2 Corinthians 4:18 says: 'So we fix our eyes not on what is seen,
> but on what is unseen. For what is seen is temporary, but what
> is unseen is eternal.' Money, a nice home, secure job, material
> things are not important. They're temporary. They won't last.
> They're not bad in themselves, but they shouldn't be what we
> base our lives around. What we should base our lives around
> is bringing God glory in everything . . . Spending time reading
> God's word and praying has been completely refreshed. It
> has a whole new 'feel' to it. I long for those times. They're
> like breath to me. Become satisfied in him! There's no better
> thing![6]

Whatever the circumstances of our lives, we have God, and knowing him eclipses everything else. The triune God himself is our reward. The Father, the Son and the Spirit are our blessing, our joy, our fullness. So 'I say to myself, "The LORD is my portion; therefore I will wait for him."'

> I waited patiently for the LORD;
>> he turned to me and heard my cry.
> He lifted me out of the slimy pit,
>> out of the mud and mire;
> he set my feet on a rock
>> and gave me a firm place to stand.
> He put a new song in my mouth,
>> a hymn of praise to our God.
> Many will see and fear the LORD
>> and put their trust in him.
> (Psalm 40:1–3)

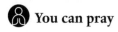 **You can pray**

A prayer based on 2 Thessalonians 2:16–17

> Our Lord Jesus Christ and God our Father,
> you have loved us.
> And by your grace
> you gave us eternal encouragement and good hope.
> Encourage our hearts and strengthen us
> in every good deed and word. Amen.

7. THE BATTLE TO PRAY – AND HOW TO WIN IT

I once heard John Stott say that the battle to pray takes place on the threshold of prayer. In other words, prayer itself is not so much the struggle. The struggle is to get down to it, to get on with it, to keep at it day after day. This is really important.

The battle is *never* that of making our prayers good enough for God. As we've seen, our prayers are *always* good prayers when offered in the name of Jesus. So there's no such thing as a good pray-er or a bad pray-er. Or rather, there is only one good pray-er and he is a *great* pray-er: the Lord Jesus Christ, who prays in eternal communion with his Father. But we pray in him. So every Christian is a great pray-er because we pray in him, and every prayer is a great prayer because we pray in him. The only question is: will I pray?

The battle is not even to keep praying for a long time. Our prayers are not more effective the longer they are. In the Bible, people are rebuked for not praying (Matthew 26:40–46; James

4:2). But no-one is rebuked for not praying for long enough. After all, what does 'long enough' actually mean? Does God time our prayers and only answer if we push past the ten-minute or the ten-hour mark? But people are rebuked for long prayers (Matthew 6:7–8). If you've already made your request, don't think you then need to find creative ways to say it again so that you can bulk up your prayers into something big enough to convince God.

No, the battle is to start praying, to get on with it, to get down to it. And this is where you and I are. Wrestling in prayer is not just something for great prayer warriors. Actually it describes your experience and mine. The main struggle is to get on with it. Often we find that, once we get going, we are blessed by the process. Stott says,

> We need to win the battle of the prayer threshold. To help me
> persevere in prayer, I sometimes imagine a very high stone wall,
> with the living God on the other side of it. In this walled garden
> he is waiting for me to come to him. There is only one way into
> the garden – a tiny door. Outside that door stands the devil with
> a drawn sword, ready to stop me. It is at this point that we need
> to defeat the devil in the name of Christ. This is the battle of the
> threshold. I think there are many of us who give up praying
> before we have even tried to fight this battle. The best way to
> win, in my experience, is to claim the promises of Scripture,
> which the devil cannot undo.[1]

Fighting the battle to pray

Prayer is hard, because we're involved in a spiritual battle, and nothing involves us in that battle more than prayer. To stop Christians praying is one of Satan's key strategies. The world, the flesh and the devil combine to distract us from prayer and discourage us in it.

But we're not alone. The world, the flesh and the devil are indeed our enemies. But we also have allies. Ephesians 6:14–20 says,

> Stand firm then, with the belt of truth buckled round your waist, with the breastplate of righteousness in place, and with your feet fitted with the readiness that comes from the gospel of peace. In addition to all this, take up the shield of faith, with which you can extinguish all the flaming arrows of the evil one. Take the helmet of salvation and the sword of the Spirit, which is the word of God.
>
> And pray in the Spirit on all occasions with all kinds of prayers and requests. With this in mind, be alert and always keep on praying for all the Lord's people. Pray also for me, that whenever I speak, words may be given me so that I will fearlessly make known the mystery of the gospel, for which I am an ambassador in chains. Pray that I may declare it fearlessly, as I should.

In the original Greek, these verses are all one long sentence. We're armed with the armour of God so that we can fight a battle that includes praying 'in the Spirit on all occasions with all kinds of prayers and requests'. It's the battle to 'be alert and always keep on praying for all the Lord's people'. Notice all the 'alls': 'all occasions', 'all kinds of prayers', 'always' and 'all the Lord's people'. Our spiritual warfare includes more than prayer. It's also about resisting temptation and maintaining unity. But prayer is up there on the frontline.

We have two allies. The first is other Christians. The word 'you' throughout these verses is plural rather than singular. Paul isn't talking to individual Christians, but the church in Ephesus as a whole. Most of the time when I pray on my own, I get distracted after about ten minutes. But praying with others is a very different experience.

Our second ally is the Holy Spirit. We pray 'in the Spirit'. The Spirit helps us resist the temptation not to pray and the Spirit helps as we pray. The armour described in Ephesians 6 is all about the truth of the gospel. The arsenal of the Spirit is the gospel. We counter the lies of Satan through the Spirit with the truth of the gospel. We may be tempted to think God will not welcome us in prayer or that he's indifferent or that other things are more enjoyable. But the belt of truth guards from these temptations. The breastplate of righteous-ness assures that, in Christ, God treats us as his children. The gospel of peace equips us to run to God. The shield of faith extinguishes Satan's attempt to persuade us that prayer is pointless. The helmet of salvation protects us from our fears. Above all, the sword of the Spirit is the word of God.

Pray at set times
The battle means that we need to plan to pray by setting aside time for prayer. We need to organize ourselves. Don Carson says, 'Much praying is not done because we do not plan to pray.'[2] Find a regular time that works for you. It may be first thing in the morning or during your commute or when you first get home from work. Jesus often 'withdrew' to pray. See if you can find somewhere away from distractions. Susanna Wesley had nineteen children, including the future preacher John Wesley and hymn-writer Charles Wesley. Surrounded by so many, she rarely had time alone, so she would lift her apron over her head to pray. Other people find it helpful to say their prayers out loud, pace up and down or write their prayers out in a journal.

Pray throughout the day
Setting aside a regular time of prayer is a great thing to do. It's like a father who makes a habit of reading his children a

story as he puts them to bed each night. But a good father wouldn't confine his relationship to those set times. Our heavenly Father delights to hear us pray at any point, not just during our set times. You might pray in odd moments here and there. I know people who spend most of the day in an ongoing conversation with God. I often use my walk to work to pray. I find it a great time for questioning prayer, in which I talk through issues with God as I walk. Here's what people said in my prayer survey:

- 'As a mother of three young kids, with lots of mundane tasks, I like to keep my whole day as an open conversation with God. I also pray with a number of friends regularly and this helps greatly to keep turning to God.'
- 'I try to pray when I think of something, right there and then. I ask for God's help when I'm frustrated or angry. I say thanks for something beautiful or joyful. I pray for someone as soon as I think of a problem they're facing. It's the habit of little one-liner prayers through the day.'
- 'When I took the bus to work every day I would pray. Now it's a habit, so that, whenever I get on a bus, I'm inclined to pray.'

Pray with others
Find someone to teach you to pray by praying with you. You'll learn as you hear them pray and discuss together how to pray for particular issues. Be a regular at your church prayer meeting. There's real power in praying together. That's my experience. I find it much easier to concentrate if I'm praying with others. And there's a power before God. In Matthew 18:19–20, God promises to hear us when two or three agree in prayer.

I know that praying aloud with others can be difficult. You feel dizzy as you start. Your words get mangled. You try to prepare what you're going to say and then lose track of what others have said. I can still remember the first time I prayed in a prayer meeting, and it felt like the room was spinning. But just give it a go. Just blurt out 'our Father' and then say whatever's on your heart. Don't worry about what other people think. I can promise you that most people will be thinking, 'It's great to hear that person praying.' And the One who really matters, your heavenly Father, always delights to hear you.

Don't wait for others at a prayer meeting. Come with a sense of responsibility for what happens. Take a lead. If there's an awkward silence, fill it. Don't be ruled by your emotions. Pray even if you don't feel like it. You've come to serve, not to be served. You may well find that rehearsing the truths of the gospel through prayer rekindles the affections of your heart. At the same time, don't *always* be the first to pray and don't pray for a long time. Give those who are more tentative an opportunity. Again, your aim is to serve rather than be served. So pray in a way that builds others up. Don't show off. Keep your prayers simple so that others can follow. Don't worry about praying polished prayers. Pray short, often and audibly.

Take up ideas from other people's prayers and develop them. This creates a sense of praying *together*. Think about a group of people talking together. If someone contributes to a conversation, they don't usually make a point that's completely unrelated to what has just been said. In the same way, create a conversation together in prayer by developing what has just been said.

Pray in an organized way

Part of Paul's call to the battle of prayer includes the call to 'always keep on praying for all the Lord's people' (Ephesians

6:18; see also 1 Thessalonians 5:17). He himself writes to the Colossians, a church he didn't found and hasn't met: 'For this reason, since the day we heard about you, we have not stopped praying for you . . .' (Colossians 1:9; Romans 1:9–10). To pray without ceasing doesn't mean we never do anything else! Rather, it means we're faithful in regularly praying for others. John Newton said, 'I count my best friends to be those who pray for me.'[3]

Reflection

Look at some of the following passages and identify for what Paul gives thanks in his prayers.

Romans 1:8–10	1 Corinthians 1:4–9
2 Corinthians 9:12–15	Ephesians 1:15–23
Philippians 1:3–6	Colossians 1:3–8
1 Thessalonians 1:2–3	1 Thessalonians 2:13–16
1 Thessalonians 3:9–13	2 Thessalonians 1:3–4
2 Timothy 1:3–5	Philemon 4–5

Not only does Paul continually pray for people, he also continually thanks God for his work in their lives. He tells the Thessalonians, 'We always thank God for all of you and continually mention you in our prayers' (1 Thessalonians 1:2). He says much the same to the Ephesians (1:16) and Colossians (1:3). Even to the church in Corinth – which caused Paul so much heartache – he writes, 'I always thank my God for you because of his grace given you in Christ Jesus' (1 Corinthians 1:4). More than anything, Paul gives thanks for faith, love and hope in people's lives, especially in the face of suffering and persecution. This is what Paul is thankful for:

- 'your faith in Christ Jesus and . . . the love you have for all God's people . . . that spring from the hope stored up for you in heaven' (Colossians 1:3–8)
- 'your faith is being reported all over the world' (Romans 1:8)
- 'your faith in the Lord Jesus and your love for all God's people' (Ephesians 1:15–16)
- 'your work produced by faith, your labour prompted by love, and your endurance inspired by hope in our Lord Jesus Christ' (1 Thessalonians 1:2–3)
- 'you received the word of God . . . as . . . the word of God . . . in all our distress and persecution . . . you are standing firm in the Lord' (1 Thessalonians 2:13–16; 3:6–9)
- 'your faith is growing more and more, and the love all of you have for one another is increasing . . . your perseverance and faith in all the persecutions and trials you are enduring' (2 Thessalonians 1:3–4)
- 'your love for all his holy people and your faith in the Lord Jesus' (Philemon 4–7)

You may find it helpful to organize the issues and people you pray for regularly. Many people use some kind of prayer diary. You could write prayer needs on cards and then pray for a few each day. Or you could use the prayer calendars which churches or mission agencies helpfully produce. Many people have a folder or a collection of papers inside their Bible. They may have a top sheet with things they pray for every day and then a collection of prayer letters, printed emails and photos, a few of which they use each day. I have an A5 book of transparent sleeves into which I insert prayer letters, prayer needs and passages of Scripture. My daughter has a pin board covered in prompts for prayer. Various apps are also available allowing you to type in prayer items (together with related prayer letters) and state how often you want to pray for that item. The app then creates daily prayer lists for you.

I also have a grid which I keep in my Bible. Across the top are the days of the week. I'm realistic about my prayer habits, so I miss out Saturday because that's when I have a lie in, and I miss out Tuesday because that's when I meet to pray with my fellow elders. In each of the remaining days, I insert members of my extended family, members of my gospel community, each of the other gospel communities in our network and missionaries connected to our church. In this way, I pray for each of them once during the week.

Here are some quotes and suggestions from my prayer survey:

- 'I keep an open diary in the kitchen at home to write down people's prayer needs and make sure they're remembered during the day as I work.'
- 'I keep a journal of prayer requests and God's responses as testimony of his faithfulness.'
- 'I've created a book with specific scriptures listed under the name of each person for whom I am praying.'

You might find it helpful to think in terms of concentric circles. Start by praying for yourself and then move out to your family, your friends and colleagues, your church and its leaders, missionaries you know, your nation and the world.

Pray the word
One of the best ways to enjoy God in prayer is 'to worship over the Bible'. Marcus Honeysett says,

> God is not glorified by us just reading the Bible. And we don't
> necessarily grow or get helped just by reading the Bible. The devil

knows the Bible – and he isn't growing as a Christian! God is
glorified when we are salivating over it and prizing its promises
and pursuing him . . . God is magnified by lives that demonstrate
that they delight in all that he is and all that he has done. That is
how he is glorified and that is how he is honoured in our Bible
reading. Therefore that is the goal of our Bible reading. So my
number-one top tip for avoiding boring Bible reading is always
this: worship over the Bible as you read it. Pray over it. We are
meant to be exposing our hearts to God so that we exult in God.
The whole point of reading the Bible is so that God gets worship
in our lives and through us to the ends of the earth.[4]

How do we do this? Read a passage. Then reread it a verse or
two at a time, turning what you read into prayer. In the case
of a story, you might focus on two or three verses that capture
your attention or summarize God's involvement. This little
rubric may help:[5]

Rejoice: What reasons does this passage highlight to
           rejoice in who God is and what God has done?
Repent: What sins does this passage highlight of which
           I need to repent?
Request: What needs does this passage highlight that I
           can turn into requests?

The great Reformer Martin Luther wrote a little book on
prayer for his barber. Maybe he was getting his hair cut one day,
and, after they finished talking about where they were going
on holiday, they started talking about prayer. The book is called
A Simple Way to Pray (1535). Luther suggests we read a passage
of Scripture and then 'fashion a garland of four strands'.[6] We
should consider first the *instruction* we find and then turn this
successively into *thanksgiving*, *confession* and *petition*.

Here are some comments from people who completed my prayer survey:

- 'I've taken to reading the same book of the Bible over and over again for one to two months. For two months, I read the book of Philippians every day. I finally know the general themes in the book and have better recall of passages.'
- 'I find it helpful to pray what I read. In other words, I read something and then respond by asking God to change me in that way!'
- 'I've been helped by thinking intentionally about what the passage says about God's character and person.'
- 'I try to come to the Bible as a sinner, ready to hear God's word – to be chastened and to feel again the great, great love of Jesus for me.'

Pray in faith for faith
James 5:16–18 says,

> The prayer of a righteous person is powerful and effective. Elijah was a human being, even as we are. He prayed earnestly that it would not rain, and it did not rain on the land for three and a half years. Again he prayed, and the heavens gave rain, and the earth produced its crops.

The phrase 'he prayed earnestly' is literally 'he prayed in his prayers'. Do you realize what that means? It means it's possible to pray without praying. We can pray as a duty, an exercise, a formality, without really praying. We need to pray in our prayers, to pour ourselves into our prayers, to pray earnestly and fervently.

How do duty and delight work in prayer? Some people stress duty. We ought to pray, so we should just get on with it. Don't worry about feelings. Do the right thing. But this can reduce prayer to a painful obligation or a work we perform to win God's reward. Other people stress delight. Prayer should be a delight, so don't make it a duty. But what do I do when prayer *isn't* a delight?

I suggest two answers. First, the Reformer John Calvin described prayer as 'the chief exercise of faith'.[7] In other words, prayer arises in our hearts as an expression of our relationship with God in Christ. Hidden in a statement like: 'I can't pray because I don't feel like praying' is an assumption that the validity of my prayer depends on my feelings. It doesn't. It depends on faith in the welcome of the Father, the mediation of the Son and the empowering of the Spirit. The key to stronger prayer is stronger faith. So then the question is: how do we strengthen our faith? Paul answers, 'Faith comes from hearing the message, and the message is heard through the word about Christ' (Romans 10:17). Our faith is strengthened as we hear and meditate on the gospel, especially in the Bible.

When prayer feels like a struggle, then turn to God's word and ask the Spirit to speak to you through it. If you're finding prayer hard going, then stop praying. Instead, open your Bible and read the word of Christ. Reflect on all he is and all he's done. Ask God to warm your heart and give you faith. Turn what you read into prayer. John Bunyan writes,

> The Holy Ghost does not immediately quicken and stir up the heart of the Christian without, but by, with, and through the Word, by bringing that to the heart, and by opening that, whereby the man is provoked to go on to the Lord, and to tell him how it is with him; and also to argue, and supplicate, according to the Word.[8]

Someone wrote in my prayer survey, 'I find that the Lord's Prayer or the Psalms act as a starter motor when I'm cold.' Another said, 'When I lived in Kenya, I attended a prayer group, and we started each session by singing and praising God (just our voices without musical instruments). It really helped draw my focus onto worshipping and talking to God. Now singing is an important part of how I communicate with God.' From time to time, I've used a 'daily office' – a traditional liturgy made up of set readings and prayers. I tend to use a modern version of the morning and evening prayer from the Book of Common Prayer.

Many people use the mnemonic 'ACTS' as a pattern for their daily prayers:

A = adoration
C = confession
T = thanksgiving
S = supplication

Start with prayers of adoration which praise God for who he is and what he's done. Then confess your sins and thank God for his mercy in Christ. Thank him, too, for specific ways in which he's blessed you or answered prayer. Then bring your needs to God, along with the needs of your family, church, mission partners and the wider world. Starting with worship in this way, as well as reminding yourself of his mercy and thanking him for his blessing, will strengthen the faith and love that underlie true prayer. This might help expand your prayers beyond a shopping list. But be careful. You don't normally structure conversations with people you love. You just talk to them about whatever is on your heart. Talking to our heavenly Father is no different.

Secondly, don't set up duty and delight as alternatives. See duty as the route to delight. *Pray in faith for faith*. It's true that duty ('bad duty', we might call it) can be a fruitless attempt to win God's approval. But duty ('good duty') can be faith saying, 'At the moment, I don't feel like praying, but I believe that God is good and, if I read his word and pray, then eventually I'll rediscover delight in him.'

As a six-year-old, I loved football. But my father loved cricket. So I can remember playing cricket with him not because I loved cricket, but because I wanted to please him. But I very quickly grew to love cricket. As a result, I spent much of my childhood throwing a ball against a wall and hitting the rebound with a stick. I would play with the cricket coverage in the background on a radio next to me. Indeed, I still keep a cricket bat in my office.

What I did at first out of duty became one of the great loves of my life. And this is how duty works in the Christian life. We pray out of duty. But, in praying, we discover a love of prayer, or rather a love of relating to God. The difference is this. Having fallen in love with cricket, I've loved it ever since. Sadly, I can't always say the same about prayer. Often I struggle. But I know that if I persist, it will lead to joy. This is faith: believing there is joy to be found through duty. The Puritans used to talk about 'praying until you pray'.[9] One of the respondents to my prayer survey said, 'I find getting started the most difficult bit, but after a few minutes, it's great.' Another reported someone as saying, 'I never feel like going to a prayer meeting, but I never leave thinking it was a waste of time.'

Better than life?
Do you remember the story of Daniel in the lions' den? Daniel's enemies pass a law saying that everyone must call on

the king. So if Daniel calls on God, he will be thrown into a den of lions. It's an attempt by the enemies of God to prevent the prayers of God's people. In the end, God closes the mouths of the lions, and Daniel is saved.

But why was Daniel thrown to the lions? Because he thought it was better to die than to give up praying to God. What about you? That battle continues today. The enemies of God still try to prevent the prayers of God's people. How hard will you fight to pray?

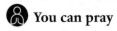 **You can pray**

A prayer based on Philippians 1:3–11

> Our God, we thank you for all those who partner with us in the
>   gospel.
> We are confident that you who began a good work in us
> will carry it on to completion until the day of Christ.
> They are in our hearts because we share together in your grace.
> You can testify how we long for them with the affection of Christ
>   Jesus.
>
> We pray that our love may abound more and more
> in knowledge and depth of insight,
> so that we may be able to discern what is best
> and may be pure and blameless for the day of Christ,
> filled with the fruit of righteousness that comes through Jesus
>   Christ
> to your glory and praise. Amen.

PART 3
WHAT WE PRAY

8. THE ARGUMENTS OF PRAYER

I wonder if your experience of prayer is a bit like this? From time to time, competitions are held in which the prize is a 'supermarket dash'. The winner keeps whatever he or she can throw into a supermarket trolley in a limited period of time. So the contestant rushes round the supermarket grabbing at this, scooping up some of that, dumping it all in the trolley before the time is up.

Sometimes our prayers can feel like that. We rush into the presence of God, grab a load of requests, dump them in our prayers and then rush out again – time is up.

Here are a couple of questions from my prayer survey:

- 'How can I move from rote prayers to reverent conversation?'
- 'How do you pray through lots of prayer requests without feeling like you're doing "shopping-list" prayers?'

In this chapter, I will look at how to argue with God. I want to encourage you not simply to state your requests: 'please do this . . .', but to present arguments to God: 'please do this because . . .' For the Bible suggests that in prayer we can really engage with God. When we read of pray-ers there, we find they are expressing a genuine relationship. And the prayers recorded in the Bible invite us not only to make our requests to God, but to present reasons why he should answer those requests. The Bible invites us, as it were, to argue with God. In Joel 2:17, we read,

> Let the priests, who minister before the LORD,
> > weep between the portico and the altar.
> Let them say, 'Spare your people, LORD.
> > Do not make your inheritance an object of scorn,
> > a byword among the nations.
> Why should they say among the peoples,
> > 'Where is their God?'

Joel is speaking on God's behalf. And he tells the people to pray for deliverance. But not only does he tell them to pray. He tells them the arguments to use. This is God telling his people what arguments to use with God!

I want to suggest there are only three arguments we can use with God in prayer, but they are very powerful. These arguments are the glory of God, the mercy of God and the promises of God. We'll find them illustrated in two Old Testament prayers.

Changing the future of a nation
In Numbers 14, the people of God rebel against Moses and Aaron, God's appointed leaders. God has led them out of slavery in Egypt and brought them to the verge of the

Promised Land. Moses has sent twelve spies to scope out the task ahead of them. The spies return with samples of the wonderful produce from the land, but also with tales of a powerful resident population. Two of the spies, Caleb and Joshua, are confident that, with God's help, they can take the land. But the other spies say, 'We can't attack those people; they are stronger than we are . . . All the people we saw there are of great size . . . We seemed liked grasshoppers in our own eyes, and we looked the same to them' (Numbers 13:31–33). At this, the people weep and complain. 'If only we had died in Egypt!' they say. 'Or in this wilderness!' 'We should choose a leader and go back to Egypt' (14:3–4). When Moses, Aaron, Caleb and Joshua try to intervene, the people talk about stoning them (14:5–10).

Then the glory of the Lord appears. The Lord speaks to Moses:

> How long will these people treat me with contempt? How long will they refuse to believe in me, in spite of all the signs I have performed among them? I will strike them down with a plague and destroy them, but I will make you into a nation greater and stronger than they.
> (Numbers 14:11–12)

You might think this would sound like an attractive option to Moses! Finally, he would be rid of this troublesome people and wouldn't have to put up with their endless grumbling any more. And all with the promise that he would be the founding father of a new nation. But instead, Moses intercedes on behalf of the people. He is a pointer to Christ, our great Mediator, who puts our salvation ahead of his own interests.

So Moses prays that God would spare the people. And he does so by employing two arguments.

1. *The glory of God*

> Moses said to the LORD, 'Then the Egyptians will hear about it! By
> your power you brought these people up from among them. And
> they will tell the inhabitants of this land about it. They have already
> heard that you, LORD, are with these people and that you, LORD,
> have been seen face to face, that your cloud stays over them, and
> that you go before them in a pillar of cloud by day and a pillar of fire
> by night. If you put all these people to death, leaving none alive, the
> nations who have heard this report about you will say, "The LORD
> was not able to bring these people into the land he promised them
> on oath, so he slaughtered them in the wilderness."'
> (Numbers 14:13–16)

Can you see Moses' argument? At the moment, the nations
are in awe of God because he's rescued Israel from Egypt and
appeared face to face with them. God has proved his power
and so brought glory to his name. But now all of this is in
jeopardy. If God destroys the Israelites, then the nations will
think he has failed.

In the same way, when Jerusalem was threatened by the
Assyrians, Hezekiah prayed, 'Now, LORD our God, deliver us
from his hand, so that all kingdoms of the earth may know that
you, LORD, are the only God' (Isaiah 37:20). The glory of God
also dominates many of Paul's prayers in the New Testament:

- 'May God . . . give you the same attitude of mind . . . so
  that with one mind and one voice you may glorify the God
  and Father of our Lord Jesus Christ' (Romans 15:5–6).
- 'Now to him who is able to do immeasurably more than
  all we ask or imagine, according to his power that is at
  work within us, to him be glory in the church and in
  Christ Jesus' (Ephesians 3:20–21).

- 'This is my prayer: that your love may abound more and more in knowledge and depth of insight . . . filled with the fruit of righteousness that comes through Jesus Christ – to the glory and praise of God' (Philippians 1:9–11).
- 'We pray this so that the name of our Lord Jesus may be glorified in you, and you in him' (2 Thessalonians 1:12).

2. *The mercy of God*

> Now may the Lord's strength be displayed, just as you have declared: 'The LORD is slow to anger, abounding in love and forgiving sin and rebellion. Yet he does not leave the guilty unpunished; he punishes the children for the sin of the parents to the third and fourth generation.' In accordance with your great love, forgive the sin of these people, just as you have pardoned them from the time they left Egypt until now.
> (Numbers 14:17–19)

Often our prayers focus on our own needs. 'We pray for Brian because he is so ill.' 'Please help me in this interview because I need a job.' In effect, we're saying that God should act because our need is great. We assume that stating our needs is reason enough for God to answer. But Moses acknowledges that God has every reason *not* to relent: he is the God who 'does not leave the guilty unpunished'. But he also points to God's great mercy: his slowness to anger, his abounding love, his forgiveness, his great love, his history of pardoning his people.

We deserve nothing from God except his wrath. We have no claims on him, no rights before him. This is why we often add 'in the name of Jesus' to the end of prayers. We have no claim on God except the mercy he has shown us in Christ.

So, as we present our requests to God, we remind him of his mercy. As we pray for ourselves, we acknowledge that we are unworthy of his blessings, but we remind him of his love and mercy. As we pray for unbelievers, we call on God to be true to his nature as the God who is slow to anger and abounding in love.

Reflection

Look at the following Bible prayers and identify what 'arguments' are used with God in these prayers.

Exodus 32:9–14
Numbers 14:10–20
Nehemiah 1:4–10
Nehemiah 9:5–37
Isaiah 37:14–20
Daniel 9:1–19

Changing the mind of a king

Daniel prays for the restoration of the Jews in Daniel 9, and his prayer leads to a change of heart by the pagan King Darius. And Daniel employs the same argument as Moses. He pleads the glory and mercy of God. But he adds a third argument: he holds God to his promises.

Daniel is living in Babylon. Nearly seventy years earlier, the Jews had been defeated by the Babylonians, and many had been taken away into exile – including the young Daniel himself. Now, many years later, Daniel reads in Jeremiah that the Jews will return to Jerusalem after seventy years. And so Daniel prays that the promise made through Jeremiah would be fulfilled.

1. *The promises of God*

> In the first year of Darius son of Xerxes (a Mede by descent),
> who was made ruler over the Babylonian kingdom – in
> the first year of his reign, I, Daniel, understood from the
> Scriptures, according to the word of the LORD given to
> Jeremiah the prophet, that the desolation of Jerusalem would
> last seventy years. So I turned to the Lord God and pleaded
> with him in prayer and petition, in fasting, and in sackcloth
> and ashes.
>
> (Daniel 9:1–3)

Daniel prayed in response to God's word for what God had
promised and what he knew to be God's will.

How are we to pray? By making sure that God's word
shapes our praying. We too pray the promises of God's
word. We should use the language of God's word, adopting
the priorities of God's word.

Above all, we should plead God's promises. When God
threatened to destroy the people of Israel after they'd built
the golden calf, Moses prayed on their behalf and reminded
God of his promises to Abraham:

> Turn from your fierce anger; relent and do not bring disaster
> on your people. Remember your servants Abraham, Isaac and
> Israel, to whom you swore by your own self: 'I will make your
> descendants as numerous as the stars in the sky and I will give
> your descendants all this land I promised them, and it will be
> their inheritance for ever.'
>
> (Exodus 32:12–13)

When Nehemiah hears about the trouble faced by the Jews
who had returned to Jerusalem, he turns to God in prayer. He

asks God to grant him favour before the Persian king. And in
his prayer, he too reminds God of his promises:

> Remember the instruction you gave your servant Moses, saying,
> 'If you are unfaithful, I will scatter you among the nations, but
> if you return to me and obey my commands, then even if your
> exiled people are at the farthest horizon, I will gather them from
> there and bring them to the place I have chosen as a dwelling for
> my Name.'
> (Nehemiah 1:8–9)

Again, in Nehemiah 9, the people pray and remind God of his
promises as they ask for his help (7–8).

The apostle John says, 'This is the confidence we have in
approaching God: that if we ask anything according to his
will, he hears us' (1 John 5:14). But how do we know what
God's will is? Christians sometimes act as if discerning God's
will is a mysterious process. It's not. 'It is a frighteningly
simple concept. Praying according to the will of God is finding
out from the Scriptures what God has promised and praying
for that.'[1] John Bunyan says, 'As the Spirit is the helper and the
governor of the soul, when it prays according to the will of
God; so it guides by and according to the Word of God and
his promises.'[2] We can pray in accordance with God's
purposes, because God has revealed his purposes in the Bible.
The promises of God are like moulds into which we pour our
prayers like liquid metal.

So we should pray with an open Bible. How else are we
going to know what to pray for? Try, for example, identifying
a verse that is relevant to each item you want to pray about
and using it to shape your requests. If you do this as a discipline
for one month, it will start to become instinctive. The priorities
of God's word will start to shape the priorities of your praying.

When we intercede, we can trust God to grant what we request because of what he has promised in his word:

- He has promised to build his church.
- He has promised to be with us always.
- He has promised that his word will not return empty.

William Gurnall said, 'Prayer is nothing but the promise reversed or God's word turned inside out and formed into an argument and retorted back again upon God by faith.'[3]

2. The mercy of God

Daniel's prayer is full of contrition. Like Moses in Numbers 14, he acknowledges that God has every reason *not* to act. Daniel 9:4–14 is a comprehensive confession of sin. The people of Israel have not obeyed God's law (verse 5) and have not listened to God's prophets (verse 6). Everyone is implicated – wherever (verse 7) and whoever (verse 8) they are. The prayer moves back and forth between the righteousness of God and the sin of the people:

> Lord, the great and awesome God, who keeps his covenant of love
> . . . we have sinned and done wrong . . . Lord, you are righteous,
> but this day we are covered with shame . . . The Lord our God is
> merciful and forgiving, even though we have rebelled against him.
> (Daniel 9:4–9)

Daniel makes no attempt to distance himself from the people's sin, even though he was only a child when he was taken into exile. 'We are covered with shame,' he says twice (verses 7, 8). As Daniel's prayer comes to its climax, he says, 'We do not make requests of you because we are righteous, but because of your great mercy' (verse 18).

In verse 16, Daniel speaks of God's 'righteous acts'. Verse 15 tells us what these are: his saving acts and the supreme act of salvation for the Old Testament people of God which was the exodus from Egypt.

> Now, Lord our God, who brought your people out of Egypt with a mighty hand and who made for yourself a name that endures to this day, we have sinned, we have done wrong. Lord, in keeping with all your righteous acts, turn away your anger and your wrath from Jerusalem, your city, your holy hill.
> (Daniel 9:15–16)

God's mercy is not some abstract notion. It's expressed in God's saving acts in history. In effect, Daniel is saying, 'Please respond to my prayer in keeping with your past merciful, righteous, saving, powerful interventions in history. Act in mercy, as you have done before.'

Paul uses the same logic in Romans 8:32: 'He who did not spare his own Son, but gave him up for us all – how will he not also, along with him, graciously give us all things?' The exodus – and especially the Passover – was a pointer to God's giving of his own Son. This is God's greatest 'righteous act'. Paul, I suspect, also had Genesis 22 in mind. Abraham stands with Isaac stretched out on the altar before him. He holds up his hand, about to strike his beloved son. Then, at the last moment, God intervenes. He stops Abraham, and Isaac is spared. An alternative is offered instead – a ram. But now another Father stands with his Son stretched out before him. He raises his hand to strike his Son, his only Son, his beloved Son. And there is no intervention, no voice from heaven, no alternative. Here on the cross God's mercy towards us is displayed in full, for all to see. Paul says of humanity that, in his wrath, 'God gave them up' (Romans 1:24, 26, 28 ESV). Now

Paul says of the Son that, in his wrath, God 'gave *him* up for us all'. What else can there be, then, that he will withhold from us?

3. *The glory of God*

> Now, our God, hear the prayers and petitions of your servant. For your sake, Lord, look with favour on your desolate sanctuary. Give ear, our God, and hear; open your eyes and see the desolation of the city that bears your Name. We do not make requests of you because we are righteous, but because of your great mercy. Lord, listen! Lord, forgive! Lord, hear and act! For your sake, my God, do not delay, because your city and your people bear your Name.
> (Daniel 9:17–19)

Why does Daniel pray? For God's sake, God's glory. Why should God respond? For the sake of his holy name, his reputation. Daniel talks about the needs of Jerusalem and the needs of the people. But they are '*your* city and *your* people'. God made a name for himself when he rescued his people from Egypt (verse 15). But now that reputation is under threat. God has attached his name to his people, and now his people have become 'an object of scorn' (verse 16). They are the city and people that 'bear *your* Name' (verse 19).

The glory of God is to be the chief end of our prayers. We should ask for that which will bring worship to God. This doesn't simply mean adding a reference to God's glory as a formulaic conclusion to our prayers. It means that every request we make should lead to the praise of God. This helps to determine for what we should pray. We can let God's glory be our guide. In any situation, we can ask ourselves: How can God be honoured? How can his reputation be extended? How can God's goodness and greatness be made clear? We should be able to say as we make our requests, 'Do this for the sake of your glory.'

The Westminster Catechism reminds us that the chief end of human beings is to glorify God and enjoy him for ever. The chief end of our praying is the same: the enjoyment of God and the glory of his name.

God-centred prayers

The promise of God, the mercy of God and the glory of God are the only arguments used by Bible pray-ers and the only arguments we can use before God. But what a trio! God himself invites us, through the Spirit-inspired examples of prayers in the Bible, to say, 'Hear our prayer because this is what you have promised. Hear our prayer because you are a merciful God. Hear our prayer because this will bring glory to your name.'

What these arguments have in common is *God*. We argue with him on the basis of *his* promises, *his* mercy and *his* glory, not on the basis of our intentions, our needs or our aspirations. Time and again, Bible prayers are thoroughly God-centred, preoccupied above all with the glory of God's name. Our prayers in contrast can often be human-centred. Many of our prayers are all about us and our needs while Bible prayers are all about God and his glory. We need to make our prayers God-centred, rather than human-centred. That doesn't mean God is glorified despite us, for his promises are fulfilled and his mercy is shown and his glory revealed in his kindness to us, as he answers our prayers.

This God-centredness means we're not manipulating God when we pray. It's not that God can be outwitted by our reasoning. These arguments focus on God himself – his faithfulness, his character, his glory. We're not persuading him to act out of character or contrary to his will. Quite the opposite. We're calling on him to be consistent with his word, his character and his intentions. We're calling on him:

- to do what he has said – to keep his promises
- to be what he is – to be merciful
- to achieve what he purposes – to glorify his name

Reflection

Think of three things for which you have recently prayed. For each one:

- Identify a Bible passage that's relevant to the issue and think how you could use it to shape your prayers.
- Think of an aspect of God's character that's relevant to this need and how this might shape your praying.
- Think how God could be glorified in the situation and how this might shape your prayers.

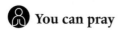 **You can pray**

A prayer based on Numbers 14:13–19

O Lord, by your power you have redeemed your people.
The nations have heard that you are with us,
that we have seen your face in Jesus Christ,
that you lead us by your Holy Spirit.
Now do not let the nations say that
     you cannot preserve your people and lead us home.
Now may your strength be displayed,
just as you have declared:

'The LORD is slow to anger,

    abounding in love and forgiving sin and rebellion.

Yet he does not leave the guilty unpunished;

      he punishes the children for the sin of the parents

      to the third and fourth generation.'

In accordance with your great love, forgive our sin,

just as you have pardoned us until now. Amen.

A prayer based on Isaiah 37:16–20

Lord Almighty, the God of Israel,

enthroned between the cherubim,

you alone are God over all the kingdoms of the earth.

You have made heaven and earth.

Give ear, Lord, and hear;

    open your eyes, Lord, and see;

listen to all the words people have sent to ridicule you,

      the living God.

Now, Lord our God, deliver your people,

so that all the kingdoms of the earth

    may know that you, Lord, are the only God. Amen.

9. THE PRIORITIES OF PRAYER: GOD'S GLORY

It's easy to know what to pray about when you face a problem: you pray about the problem. But what about when you sit down to pray in the morning. Where do you begin? You could pray for anything, but 'anything' is a big agenda to follow! What should be the priorities of our prayers?

The disciples ask Jesus, 'Lord, teach us to pray' (Luke 11:1). Jesus responds with a model prayer, commonly called 'the Lord's Prayer'. He says, 'When you pray, say . . .' This suggests he anticipates people using the very words he gives. So it's appropriate for Christians to repeat this prayer together in a liturgical way. At the same time, there are some variations between the two accounts of the Lord's Prayer in Matthew 6:9–13 and Luke 11:2–4. These differences suggest Jesus gave different forms of this teaching on prayer in different contexts, and that what matters is not a specific form of words, but following the pattern. The Lord's Prayer offers a great framework for praying. You can take each line and expand on it with your own praise and requests. Let's do this together.

Our Father in heaven

Matthew 6:9	**Luke 11:2**
Our Father in heaven	Father

What's a good prayer and what's a bad prayer? I'm always reluctant to 'correct' specific prayers, because prayer is the last place where I want people feeling self-conscious. There's a freedom of speech in prayer, because we have a Father who responds wisely to our requests, and we have the mediation of Christ and the Spirit who intercedes for us in accordance with God's will.

Yet in Matthew 6, Jesus does 'correct' prayer. He does identify two types of wrong prayers. But he's not correcting what people say, rather the reason why they say it.

1. *Praying to impress other people*. This is the danger of the Pharisees (the 'hypocrites'):

> And when you pray, do not be like the hypocrites, for they love to pray standing in the synagogues and on the street corners to be seen by others. Truly I tell you, they have received their reward in full. But when you pray, go into your room, close the door and pray to your Father, who is unseen. Then your Father, who sees what is done in secret, will reward you.
> (Matthew 6:5–6)

Whatever words they might use to address God, their audience is not actually God, but other people. And these prayers work: 'they have received their reward in full.' But the problem is that they only achieve the rather limited aim of impressing other people.

Such prayers don't impress God. When Jesus tells us to pray in secret, however, he's not banning public prayer. All through the Bible, people pray together and are encouraged to do so. Instead, Jesus is using the image of the private room to convey the idea that we pray to God rather than to impress other people. No-one sees your private prayers. There's no motive for praying in private other than to know God better and plead for his glory.

Public prayer is different. When you pray in a prayer meeting or a church gathering you're serving the whole group. You're praying on behalf of everyone. What you say needs to be a prayer they can understand and to which they can say 'Amen'. So private prayers and public prayers will be different in style. My private prayers, for example, often feel more conversational than my public prayers. But if your public prayers are impassioned and your private prayers are perfunctory, then something is clearly wrong.

2. *Praying to impress God.* This is the danger of the pagans.

> And when you pray, do not keep on babbling like pagans, for they think they will be heard because of their many words. Do not be like them, for your Father knows what you need before you ask him.
> (Matthew 6:7–8)

This is a form of manipulation or bargaining. If I pray well or long enough, I suppose, then God will be bound to answer. It's as if we can nag God into submission. But

our God is a sovereign God who can't be coerced
through our prayers and a gracious God who doesn't
need to be coerced through our prayers.

Imagine two people praying. The prayer of one is
short and stumbling. The other's prayer is long and
eloquent. Which is better? The striking thing is that
Jesus says, *the wrong prayer is the long prayer*. A
characteristic of Christian prayer is brevity. 'Your
Father knows what you need before you ask him'
(Matthew 6:8). We don't have to inform God through
our prayers. We can't manipulate him through long
prayers. Prayer is not like a fund-raising thermometer.
We don't have to pile up our prayers until we hit the
target and God finally acts. Of course, there's nothing
intrinsically wrong with long or eloquent prayers.
The real problem is trying to impress God or other
people.

This is why the opening line of the Lord's Prayer is so
important: 'Our Father in heaven'. This is the antidote to
prayers designed to impress. Straight away, we're reminded
that God is gracious ('our Father') and sovereign ('in heaven').
He is, as we've seen, the loving Father who delights to hear
his children and give us good gifts (Luke 11:5–13).

Your relationship with your boss depends on the success of
your work. Your relationship with a judge depends on whether
or not you're guilty. Your relationship with a teacher depends
on how hard you work in lessons. In each case, their approval
depends on performance. But your relationship with your
father should be very different. He still cares about your performance; he wants you to do well at school or at work. But
his love doesn't depend on this. He's not going to sack you
as his child! Indeed, his love is often evoked when you face

problems. My wife and I often commented that our teenage girls were delightful young women everywhere except at home. Everywhere else, they were on their best behaviour. Sometimes we could almost see them finding it exhausting. But when they were at home, they could kick off their shoes and be themselves – not always with pleasant results. They were totally confident in our parental love, so they didn't have to perform. Your Father in heaven wants you to live a life that will glorify his Son. But his love doesn't depend on your performance and neither does his response to your prayers. He loves you as his child because he loves you in his own beloved Son.

Some people feel they can't approach God as Father because their own father was distant or cruel or absent. This can be a real difficulty. A friend's mother had an alcoholic father who was often abusive. As a result, she finds it impossible to think of God as a Father. But think of it like this. The very fact that we're disappointed or angry with our own fathers reveals that we know what a good father should be like. God is the Father you always wished you had.

There are many ways in which we can *address* God. But, whatever words we might use, we can only *approach* him as Father. In Acts 4:24, for example, the church addresses God as 'Sovereign Lord'. That was appropriate because they were facing persecution. Their prayer asserts that God is sovereign, even in their suffering. But if you only thought of God as the Sovereign Lord, you would be too afraid to approach him in prayer. It's only because you know him as your Father that you can approach the Sovereign Lord.

So relish the words: 'our Father'. Meditate on the privilege of calling God 'my Father'. Let the words roll round your mouth as if you were sucking on a sweet: 'our Father in heaven'.

Hallowed be your name

Matthew 6:9	**Luke 11:2**
Hallowed be your name	Hallowed be your name

'Hallowed' isn't a word we often use today. It simply means 'holy' or 'set apart'. We're praying that God's name might be holy. Clearly, we're not praying for some kind of improvement in God's character. God can't be more perfect than he already is. Instead, we're praying that his name would be *recognized* as holy. We talk about someone having a good or a bad name. It's a way of talking about their reputation. When we pray, 'Hallowed by your name', we're praying for God's reputation, that he would be honoured and glorified.

God called his people in the Old Testament to live in such a way that the nations would see that God is good and that it's good to live under his rule. God's people were to be holy as God is holy, and so reveal the holiness of his name to the nations. But instead, they followed the ways of the nations, damaging God's reputation through their evil. So God exiled them in order to protect the holiness of his name. He disassociated himself from the evil of his people by judging them. But this created a new threat to his reputation. Ezekiel 36:20 says, 'Wherever they went among the nations they profaned my holy name, for it was said of them, "These are the LORD's people, and yet they had to leave his land."' It looked as if God couldn't look after his people. So, through Ezekiel, God says to Israel,

> It is not for your sake, people of Israel, that I am going to do these things, but for the sake of my holy name, which you have profaned among the nations where you have gone. I will show the holiness of my great name, which has been profaned among

the nations, the name you have profaned among them. Then the
nations will know that I am the LORD, declares the Sovereign
LORD, when I am proved holy through you before their eyes.
(Ezekiel 36:22–23)

God hallows his name both in judgment and in salvation. So
what are we praying when we say, 'Hallowed be your name'?

- We're praying for ourselves as God's people, that our
  lives and our life together as God's covenant people
  might bring glory to God.
- We're praying that God would intervene in history to
  save people, so that they join us in worshipping his name.
- We're praying that God would intervene to bring
  history to an end with the final judgment, so that his
  name is vindicated.

This is a dangerous prayer to pray. It might lead to radical
change in your life. God might take something from you that's
a rival for your heart's affections. And one day, this prayer will
bring history to an end. One day, this prayer will mean all who
have despised God's name will be judged unless they've first
called on the name of Jesus for salvation.

Your kingdom come, your will be done

Matthew 6:10	Luke 11:2
your kingdom come,	your kingdom come
your will be done,	
on earth as it is in heaven	

The kingdom of God was the central theme of Jesus' proclamation. He began his ministry 'proclaiming the good news of

God'. 'The time has come,' he said. 'The kingdom of God has come near. Repent and believe the good news!' (Mark 1:14–15). To understand what this means, we need to go back to the beginning of the story. God made humanity to live in his world under his rule, a rule of justice, peace and love that brings freedom, joy and blessing. Adam lived under God's good rule by trusting his word, specifically the command not to eat from the tree of the knowledge of good and evil. But Satan led Adam and Eve to doubt God's word and so reject God's rule. Satan portrayed God as a tyrant, holding humanity back through his restrictive rule. To this day, people believe this lie and so reject God's rule. But the result is not that humanity found freedom, but that we lost it, becoming enslaved to sin and self. And when my kingdom encounters your kingdom, the result is conflict. Moreover, God was not dethroned by our rebellion. He remained King. The difference is that we now experience his rule as judgment.

But God is gracious. He promised that he would provide a Saviour to restore his good rule over a new humanity and save them from his own judgment. Israel was to model this promised rule in their life as God's people. God promised that their King would be the One through whom God would restore his good rule over the world. Now Jesus declares that God's kingdom is coming. He himself is God's King.

But there's a surprise. The miracles of Jesus clearly demonstrate his authority as King, and wonderfully anticipate the new world that God will create. But his coming doesn't match Jewish expectation of God's kingdom. There's no blaze of glory, no army of angels. Instead, his authority is contested, and the Roman occupiers of the Promised Land are not defeated.

In Matthew 13 and Mark 4, Jesus explains what's happening through a series of parables. The kingdom comes in two stages. It comes, for example, as a small seed that will grow into a tree encompassing the whole earth. One day, the kingdom will come as the Jews expected, in great glory, and bring judgment on God's enemies. The problem is that everyone is God's enemy, for everyone is a rebel against his rule. So first God's kingdom comes in a secret way, in grace through the word of God as the offer of salvation, in the person of Jesus. At the first coming of Jesus, judgment doesn't fall. Or rather, it falls in the most unexpected way. It falls not on *God's enemies*, but on *God's King*. Jesus himself is judged at the cross in the place of his people. He bears the penalty we deserve, so that we can be acquitted and forgiven.

The resurrection and ascension of Jesus are the declaration by God that Jesus is the world's Lord and King. Jesus ascends through the clouds into heaven to receive an eternal kingdom. In the light of this authority over the nations, he sends out his disciples to call the nations to obey his rule. As he has always done from creation onwards, God continues to rule through his word. So the kingdom of God advances through the proclamation of the gospel word, whenever we tell people Jesus is their King, every time someone submits to Jesus as their Lord.

One day, Jesus will return from heaven to renew this world and restore God's rule. Heaven and earth will be united, and creation will be made new. Those who believe the gospel will experience his coming rule as one of justice, peace and love that brings freedom, joy and blessing – just as Adam and Eve did in the garden, only more so. But those who have rejected the gospel will experience his coming rule as judgment and defeat.

This story reveals what we're asking for when we pray, 'Your kingdom come, your will be done on earth as it is in heaven.' We're praying:

- For ourselves, that our lives and our life together as God's people might increasingly be lived in obedience to his rule, that we might do God's will just as it is done in heaven.
- For our mission, that God would give us opportunities and make us bold so we can proclaim that Jesus is King to a rebellious world.
- For other people, that they might submit to Jesus as Lord, and find freedom and forgiveness under his rule.
- For the return of Jesus, the final restoration of God's kingdom over all the earth and the renewal of creation. We're praying that the complete obedience to God's will in heaven would become a reality on earth as well.

Bigger prayers and bigger lives

The first half of the Lord's Prayer focuses on God and his glory. We begin with: 'your name . . . your kingdom . . . your will'. This is our priority in prayer, for this is our priority in life.

I want to make two assertions.

First, you can pray for whatever you want. There are no wrong requests in prayer. Why? Because God welcomes us as a gracious Father and answers us as a wise Father. If your four-year-old child wants to pray for her hamster, then her heavenly Father delights to hear that prayer. If you want to pray for a Ferrari, then your heavenly Father delights to hear that prayer (though in his wisdom he might not give you what you ask).

Secondly, your prayers should be shaped by biblical priorities. Their concern should be the hallowing of God's name and the coming of his kingdom. You should be praying, 'Your will, not my will, be done.'

How do we account for the apparent contradiction between these two assertions? Can we pray for what we want or must we pray with biblical priorities? The answer is that Christian maturity involves narrowing the gap between what I want and what God wants. My priorities become more aligned with his priorities.

This works in both directions. The priorities of my life will increasingly be reflected in my prayer requests. At the same time, what I pray will shape the priorities of my life. This will be especially true if my prayers are shaped by the Lord's Prayer and the other prayers of the Bible. You can't pray the Lord's Prayer each day – not with any meaning – without it recalibrating your life.

Praying the Lord's Prayer will create something like a Copernican revolution. Nicolaus Copernicus was the sixteenth-century astronomer who demonstrated that the earth revolved around the sun rather than the sun revolving round the earth. This discovery was revolutionary (in more ways than one). In the same way, human beings naturally assume the world revolves around them. We even treat God as if he revolves around us, as if he's there to meet our needs. But it's we who revolve around him. He's at the centre, and his glory should be our main concern.

What does this look like? Can I still pray for my headache? Yes, but you pray for it in a God-centred way. Your request should be shaped by God's priorities. You might pray that God will heal you, but that, if he doesn't, you would still be enabled to glorify him in your pain.

In some ways, we only ever have one prayer: 'Hallowed be your name and your kingdom come.' But we make this request in a thousand different contexts. Are you praying for a missionary your church supports? Pray that God would glorify his name and extend his kingdom through their ministry. Are you praying for a Christian friend in hospital? Pray that their attitude to their illness would glorify God. Are you praying for your finances? Pray that God would glorify his name by providing for your needs. Are you praying for the day ahead? Pray that you would glorify God in all you do, and that he would give you opportunities to proclaim his kingdom.

This also helps us to accept unanswered prayer. When you're praying for bigger goals, you see unanswered prayers in a different light. Let's suppose you're praying for a friend to be healed. If he was healed, people would be very excited and praise God. For a couple of months. But soon it would be old news. Suppose your friend isn't healed, but instead responds to his suffering with faith and hope. Week after week his witness would bring glory to God.

An elderly lady in our church had acute arthritis for many years. Yet she was always full of joy in Christ. So week after week, she caused me to praise God. Week after week, his name was glorified in her life. About that time, someone else in our church was diagnosed with terminal cancer. We discussed together how we should pray for her. We agreed to pray for God to be glorified in her illness and for her testimony to her two unbelieving children. God answered that prayer. Her faith in the face of death had a profound impact in the hospital where she eventually died, and her two children were converted.

Reflection

1. List some typical prayer requests from your personal and church prayer times.
2. Read Colossians 1:9–14. List all the things that Paul prays for the Colossian Christians.
3. Read Colossians 4:2–6. For what does Paul request prayer?

4. What are the similarities and differences between your prayer requests and Paul's?

5. Look at some of Paul's other prayers and prayer requests. For what does Paul normally pray?

Romans 15:5–6, 13, 30–33	2 Corinthians 13:14
Ephesians 1:17–19	Ephesians 3:16–21
Ephesians 6:18–20	Philippians 1:9–11
1 Thessalonians 3:9–13	2 Thessalonians 1:11–12
2 Thessalonians 2:16–17	2 Thessalonians 3:16
1 Timothy 2:1–7	Philemon 4–6

6. Choose three things about which you want to pray. Consider how Paul might pray for them.

We find the same big vision in Paul's prayers. Throughout his letters, there are *reports* of prayers and *requests* for prayer. They teach us a lot about his priorities. They reveal a God-centred vision of life, and a passion for extending God's kingdom in the lives of Christians and through us in proclamation to the lost. They're a great model. Read through this summary of Paul's reports of prayer and requests for prayer. Reflect on the extent to which your life and your prayers reflect these priorities.

Romans 10:1
- that people may be saved

Romans 15:5–6, 13, 30–33
- that Christians may be united
- that Christians may be full of joy, peace and hope
- that Christians may be kept safe from persecution
- that Christians may be reconciled across ethnic divides

2 Corinthians 13:14
- that Christians might share the grace of Christ, the love of God and the community of the Spirit

Ephesians 1:15–23
- that Christians may know God better through his Spirit
- that Christians may know the riches of our glorious hope
- that Christians may know God's power in our lives

Ephesians 3:14–21
- that Christians may have power so Christ may dwell in our hearts
- that Christians may have power to grasp the extent of Christ's love

Ephesians 6:19–20
- that Christians may have the courage to proclaim the gospel

Philippians 1:9–11
- that our love may increasingly be shaped by the gospel
- that Christians may be blameless when Christ returns
- that Christians may be filled with the fruit of righteousness
- that Christians may bring praise and glory to God

Colossians 1:9–14
- that Christians may know God's will through the Spirit
- that Christian lives may be worthy of God and pleasing to God
- that Christians may bear fruit, grow in knowledge, have power to endure and give thanks with joy

Colossians 4:2–4
- that Christians may have opportunities to proclaim the gospel
- that Christians may proclaim the gospel clearly

1 Thessalonians 3:10–13
- that Christians may have opportunities to build up one another's faith
- that the love of Christians may increase
- that Christians may be blameless when Christ returns

1 Thessalonians 5:23–24
- that Christians may be sanctified
- that Christians may be blameless when Christ returns

2 Thessalonians 1:11–12
- that Christians may be worthy of our calling
- that the work our faith prompts us to do may bear fruit
- that Christians may glorify Jesus and enjoy his glory

2 Thessalonians 2:16–17
- that Christians may be encouraged and strengthened in good works and words

1 Timothy 2:1–7
- that people may be saved
- that political authorities may allow Christians the freedom to proclaim the gospel

If you live for your kingdom, then you'll live in a small world and pray small prayers. Your concern will be your will and your needs. Your prayers will rarely extend beyond your garden fence. Small prayers for a small person. But when you live for God's kingdom, then you live in a big world and pray big prayers. Even the minutiae of your life become profoundly significant because your concern is the glory of God in everything. Your prayers will range across the world because your passion will be to see God's name proclaimed to all nations. We need to pray bigger prayers, prayers that move beyond our world into God's.

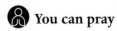 **You can pray**

The Lord's Prayer (based on Matthew 6:9–13 and Luke 11:2–4)
We'll be exploring the second half of the Lord's Prayer in the next chapter, when it will again be the prayer at the end of the chapter. So when you take each line as a starting point for praise and prayer, focus on the first four lines in this chapter and the second half in the next. The version below is the modern liturgical version.

> Our Father in heaven,
> hallowed be your name.
> Your kingdom come,
> your will be done on earth as in heaven.
> Give us today our daily bread.
> Forgive us our sins,
> as we forgive those who sin against us.
> Lead us not into temptation,
> but deliver us from evil.
> For the kingdom, the power and the glory are yours.
> Now and for ever. Amen.

10. THE PRIORITIES OF PRAYER: OUR NEEDS

How should we pray for ourselves? Indeed, can we pray for ourselves, or is that selfish? If the priority of our prayers is to be the glory of God, then is there any room left for my concerns?

As we have seen, the first half of the Lord's Prayer focuses on God's glory. In the second half, Jesus invites us to focus on our needs:

- for provision ('give us today our daily bread')
- for pardon ('forgive us our sins')
- for protection ('lead us not into temptation')

This doesn't mean that we've left God and his glory behind. To pray for our daily bread is an act of worship, because implicit in it is an assertion that God is *a gracious Father* who *wants* to give good gifts and *a sovereign Father* who *can* give good gifts to his children (Luke 11:13). Of course, it is possible to pray in a way that's greedy or selfish (Ezekiel 33:31; James 4:3). But that doesn't mean we can't pray for what we need or what we want. If it's legitimate for us to have something, then it's legitimate for us to pray for it. God is glorified when we ask for things, because we're treating him as the generous, capable Father that he is.

Give us today our daily bread

Matthew 6:11	**Luke 11:3**
Give us today our daily bread	Give us each day our daily bread

It's easy to see how significant this request was in Jesus' day. There were no fridges or freezers, so food wouldn't keep. Praying for bread each day made sense because bread was a daily acquisition. Most people were either small-scale farmers or day labourers. If you were a farmer, then your provision was dependent on your harvests. If you were a day labourer, then you lived from day to day. Life was precarious. In Acts, we read of famine across the Roman world (Acts 11:27–30).

Life for us in the West is very different. Most of us have food in our cupboards and money in the bank. Life is not so precarious. We're confident that we'll eat tomorrow. So is this request now redundant? Why should I pray for bread today when I already have cupboards full of food?

I suggest that we need to pray this prayer as much as ever, precisely because we no longer feel so dependent. This prayer is a reminder that we can't take life for granted. We *are* dependent on God, just as much as in first-century Palestine. The economic systems of the Western world might hide this, but the reality remains the same. God sustains all life through his providential care (Psalm 65). Each breath we take comes from him. Jesus holds everything together by his word (Hebrews 1:3). Without God's continual intervention, the atoms of your body would collapse into nothing. All the blessings we enjoy are a gift from God. We're to pray for our daily bread because we depend on God and because we need to *recognize* that we depend on him.

Our daily need for food is a reminder that we're finite. We may eat and be full, but a few hours later we're hungry again. We're not self-sufficient. We need the help of other people. Food reminds us that we are part of a wider community: farmers, producers, manufacturers, transporters, retailers, cooks and so on. And it reminds us that we need God.

Our lives are just as precarious, whether we recognize it or not. My friend has started his own business. The early days were anxious times for him. Often he worried about whether he would have enough money in the bank. A few years on and the business has grown. He now employs eight staff members and his turnover has increased tenfold. But the worries haven't gone away. All he's done is add a zero to the money he needs each month to pay his workers. His worries have increased.

We may have food in our cupboards, but we still have plenty to worry about: our jobs, our futures, our income, our health, our children, our retirement, our safety. Jesus goes on in Matthew's Gospel to elaborate on this request from the Lord's Prayer when he says, 'Do not worry about your life' (Matthew 6:25). What's his antidote to anxiety?

First, Jesus warns us not to store up treasure on earth because earthly treasure brings with it worry. That's its real price tag. 'Do not store up for yourselves treasures on earth,' he says, 'where moths and vermin destroy, and where thieves break in and steal' (Matthew 6:19). If you buy a flashy new car, then you'll start to worry about it being stolen. If you buy a beautiful new carpet, then you'll worry about it being stained. If you buy a trendy new gadget, then you'll worry about it becoming outdated. If you invest your money, then you'll worry about the stock market falling. Instead, says Jesus, 'store up for yourselves treasures in heaven, where moths and vermin do not destroy, and where thieves do not break in and steal' (Matthew 6:20). A totally secure investment that pays eternal dividends.

Secondly, Jesus invites us to trust our heavenly Father. 'Therefore I tell you, do not worry about your life, what you will eat or drink; or about your body, what you will wear. Is not life more than food, and the body more than clothes?' (Matthew 6:25). Jesus invites us to consider flowers: you stick them in a vase and a few days later throw them away. Yet God clothes them with such intricate beauty. How much more will he care for his children! What is Jesus' conclusion?

> So do not worry, saying, 'What shall we eat?' or 'What shall we drink?' or 'What shall we wear?' For the pagans run after all these things, and your heavenly Father knows that you need them. But seek first his kingdom and his righteousness, and all these things will be given to you as well. Therefore do not worry about tomorrow, for tomorrow will worry about itself. Each day has enough trouble of its own.
> (Matthew 6:31–34)

Notice how closely this exhortation ties into the Lord's Prayer.

Matthew 6:5–13	Matthew 6:31–34
'Our Father in heaven'	'Your heavenly Father'
'Your Father knows what you need before you ask him.'	'Your heavenly Father knows that you need them.'

'Your kingdom come.'	'But seek first his kingdom.'
'Give us today our daily bread.'	'Therefore do not worry about tomorrow, for tomorrow will worry about itself. Each day has enough trouble of its own.'

What's the significance of this connection? We're to present our concerns and needs to God our Father in prayer. Doing so will help to free us from worry. They become God's problem rather than ours! This sets us free to seek his kingdom today. We can make his kingdom our priority because we trust him to provide for our needs. We're back to the concerns in the first half of the Lord's Prayer. To pray, 'Give us today our daily bread', is to pray that we might be liberated to seek first God's kingdom. We let God worry about tomorrow while we serve him today. We let him care for our needs while we seek his kingdom. This liberated and liberal service of God is rooted in the confidence that he's our Father in heaven, our gracious and sovereign Father who will care for us just as he cares for flowers.

Recently I visited a couple who both work part-time so they have time for mission among one of the ethnic groups in our city. The reason for my visit was that a few days earlier, they'd been burgled. All their spare money was going on fixing their new home, so this was a big blow. They were at the end of their emotional and financial resources. I went to encourage them. But I came away encouraged myself and even challenged, for they were full of joy and stories of God's goodness.

They'd been sleeping on an airbed for several months because they were unable to afford a mattress. When a friend heard this, he gave them a gift of money. Then the father of one of their contacts wrote from Central Asia with another money gift. They discovered that a Christmas decoration they'd been given actually contained a roll of cash. They were emptying some boxes and found an envelope with still more money. By this point, they were dancing round the kitchen celebrating God's generosity. 'Let's open this drawer,' they were joking to one another. 'Perhaps God's put some money in it for us.' They had enough money to buy a good mattress. But what about what had been stolen? In the same week, the husband's father phoned to say he'd got a spare laptop from his company for them. When it arrived, it turned out to be a much better model. Another family member sent her old smartphone. Two days after the break-in, the wife was in tears after all the emotional strain. Her husband wanted to treat her, but they had no money. So he prayed to God. That day he won cinema tickets at a work function.

'This is the way we want to live,' they said, 'not relying on ourselves, but looking to God to provide day by day. We've been so blessed through our burglary! We've seen God being so generous to us.'

They're not looking to God to make their life comfortable. They've made many sacrifices to seek first his kingdom. It means they feel very dependent on him. But it also means they see every blessing in their life as a gift from him, they see God at work day by day. This creates a life in which you can dance round the kitchen with joy, expecting money to appear in drawers.

If you want to know the provision of your Father, then put yourself in situations where you need him as you seek first his kingdom. Pray, 'Your kingdom come.' We can make our lives very safe and then wonder why we never see God delivering us. We can organize ministry so that we're self-reliant and then wonder why we never see the Spirit acting in power. We can leave no space for the Spirit to work and then wonder why he never turns up.

My friends told me, 'Every night we'll sleep on a mattress that was God's gift to us.'

My mattress is a gift from him as well. But their choice to seek first his kingdom and their prayer for daily needs make this gift of a mattress much more meaningful to them. Blessing is theirs. This prayer will change your life too.

Forgive us our debts

Matthew 6:12	**Luke 11:4**
And forgive us our debts, as we also have forgiven our debtors	Forgive us our sins, for we also forgive everyone who sins against us

With the next line of the Lord's Prayer, we move from our physical to our spiritual needs. And top of the list is our need for forgiveness. If you're a Christian, it's not that you're unforgiven until you pray this prayer. This petition comes towards the end of the prayer. So it's not that we have to regain God's forgiveness before we can move on to anything else. We already have his acceptance in Christ. The Father loved us before the creation of the world in Christ and that's why he sent his Son to atone for our sins. We've already said, 'Our Father'. We come as the children in whom he delights and whom he delights to hear.

We pray, 'Forgive us our sins', for three reasons. First, to restore the relationship. God doesn't love us any less when we sin, nor does he hold us at arm's length. But we're holding him at arm's length, pushing him away, replacing him at the centre of our lives, in the affections of our hearts. When we sin, we're saying that something matters more to us than God and his glory. So we come asking for forgiveness. We leave our sin behind and come back to God.

Secondly, we pray for forgiveness to restore our assurance. When we pray, 'Forgive us our debts', we hear his gracious word of forgiveness. We might not hear it audibly, but we hear by faith in his word. 1 John 1:9, for example, says, 'If we confess our sins, he is faithful and just and will forgive us our sins and purify us from all unrighteousness.' I could give a thousand other examples from the Bible. Psalm 103:10–12 says,

> He does not treat us as our sins deserve
> > or repay us according to our iniquities.
> For as high as the heavens are above the earth,
> > so great is his love for those who fear him;
> as far as the east is from the west,
> > so far has he removed our transgressions from us.

An unrepentant Christian can have no assurance. He or she may be saved. Or they may not be saved. We can't be sure. That individual can't be sure. But *anyone* who comes to Christ in faith and repentance hears his word of promise: 'Whoever comes to me I will never drive away' (John 6:37). The act of seeking God's forgiveness is the confirmation of his gracious work in my life.

Thirdly, we pray for forgiveness to remind us that we're to be a forgiving community. The Lord's Prayer says, 'And forgive us our debts, as we also have forgiven our debtors' (Matthew 6:12). Jesus expands on this immediately after the prayer: 'For if you forgive other people when they sin against you, your heavenly Father will also forgive you. But if you do not forgive others their sins, your Father will not forgive your sins' (Matthew 6:14–15).

It's not that we earn God's forgiveness by being forgiving. The direction is the other way round. We become forgiving people as we receive forgiveness from God. But this does mean that our forgiveness is *a sign* of his forgiveness in our lives. It's doubtful whether an unforgiving person really knows God's forgiveness. To the extent that we realize the depth of God's grace, we too will be gracious.

Peter asks Jesus how often we should forgive someone who keeps sinning against us (Matthew 18:21–35). Peter suggests that maybe seven times would be a generous figure. But Jesus responds with seventy-seven (or, in some versions, seventy times seven). In other words, there should be no limit. Why? Because there's no limit to God's forgiveness. Jesus goes on to tell the parable of a man who's forgiven a huge debt by the king. It's a picture of our huge debt of sin that God has forgiven. But in the parable, this man then imprisons someone who owes him a small debt. When the king hears about his lack of mercy, he has him thrown into prison. The warning is not to be like this man: to be recipients of God's mercy who are not then merciful people ourselves.

Luke tells a real-life story of a religious leader called Simon who invites Jesus for dinner, but proves to be a *poor host*. The meal is gatecrashed by a notoriously sinful woman who washes the feet of Jesus, dries them with her hair and anoints them with oil. This gatecrasher proves to be the *true host*. Simon is scandalized, but Jesus says, 'I tell you, her many sins have been forgiven – as her great love has shown. But whoever has been forgiven little loves little' (Luke 7:47). Our generosity to others is a sure-fire indication of the extent to which we have grasped God's generosity to us.

A few years ago, I pastored a man who lacked any assurance of salvation. As we talked, it became clear this was because he couldn't forgive. He had in mind specific crimes committed by specific people. Every time we talked, the conversation would circle back to these people. His problem was that, in his heart of hearts, he knew that the criteria he used to judge these people condemned him as well. And so he knew no assurance of God's forgiveness. When I spoke of God's grace, he hated it. He didn't like a God who would so readily forgive those who'd hurt him. It felt too high a price to pay for his own forgiveness. The journey to forgiveness and freedom involved many small steps. But the more he knew himself forgiven, the more forgiving he became. Eventually, he sought reconciliation, but it was a long and bumpy road.

This certainly applies to our attitude towards those who have wronged us. But Jesus' vision is even bigger. In Matthew's version we pray, 'Forgive us our debts, as we also have forgiven our debtors' (Matthew 6:12). 'Our debts' are clearly a picture of our sin, our unpaid obligations towards God. But why not speak directly of sin? Why speak of debts? Luke's version is even more pointed. Literally, what Jesus says is: 'Forgive us our sins, for we also forgive our debtors.' Because God forgives us our sins, we forgive our debtors.

Jesus' first listeners would have thought straight away of the jubilee laws in the law of Moses. Deuteronomy 15:1, for example, says, 'At the end of every seven years you must cancel debts.' In the same way, the Israelites were to release slaves every seventh year. Why? 'Remember that you were slaves in Egypt and the LORD your God redeemed you. That is why I give you this command today' (Deuteronomy 15:15). Their experience of liberation was to make them a liberating people. And our experience of grace is to make us a gracious community.

The Lord's Prayer is both a request and a reminder that our church communities are to be jubilee communities of generosity and grace. They're to model a different kind of economics. They're to be places where 'there need be no poor people among you' (Deuteronomy 15:4; Acts 4:33–35).

We can be generous because God is generous towards us, a gracious Father who provides for our daily need:

> There need be no poor people among you, for in the land the LORD your God is giving you to possess as your inheritance, he will richly bless you . . . Give generously to [the poor] and do so without a grudging heart; then because of this the LORD your God will bless you in all your work and in everything you put your hand to.
> (Deuteronomy 15:4, 10)

Again, think how radically this prayer changes those who truly pray it!

Lead us not into temptation

Matthew 6:13	Luke 11:4
And lead us not into temptation, but deliver us from the evil one	And lead us not into temptation

In making this request, we're not praying that we'll never be tempted. Temptation is the common experience of Christians. 1 Corinthians 10:13 says, 'The temptations in your life are no different from what others experience' (NLT).

We're praying, instead, that we might not face temptation that we can't endure. 1 Corinthians 10:13 continues, 'God is faithful; he will not let you be tempted beyond what you can bear. But when you are tempted, he will also provide a way out so that you can endure it.' We're praying for the fulfilment of this promise – that God will not let us face temptation we can't bear, and that instead he will provide a way of escape and empower us to take it.

The word 'temptation' can also be translated 'trial' or 'test'. It's the word used in the Greek version of the Old Testament to describe Israel's temptation in the wilderness. Moses says, 'Remember how the LORD your God led you all the way in the wilderness these forty years, to humble and *test* you in order to know what was in your heart, whether or not you would keep his commands' (Deuteronomy 8:2; see also Exodus 15:25; 16:4; 20:20; Deuteronomy 4:34; 13:3; Judges 2:20 – 3:4).

The Israelites failed that test. They didn't trust God. God rescued them from Egypt, dramatically defeating the gods of Egypt and parting the Red Sea. He led them through the wilderness, providing bread from heaven and water from the rock. Yet, as they stood on the verge of the Promised Land, they were too afraid of its inhabitants to enter. They didn't trust God to give them victory and fulfil his promises. The writer of Hebrews says we stand in the same situation. The Israelites didn't enter God's rest because of their unbelief (Hebrews 3:16–18).

> Therefore, since the promise of entering his rest still stands, let us be careful that none of you be found to have fallen short of it. For we also have had the good news proclaimed to us, just as they did; but the message they heard was of no value to them, because they did not share the faith of those who obeyed.
> (Hebrews 4:1–2)

Like the first generation of Israel who were rescued from Egypt, we've heard the promises of God in the gospel. The warning to us is not to fall away like they did. This is what we pray when we say, 'Lead us not into temptation.' We're asking that we might not be like the Israelites who were redeemed from Egypt, but didn't have faith in God's promises. Over a period of forty years, they died in the desert. We're praying that we might have persevering faith.

In this, we have great hope. Both Matthew and Luke describe Jesus being tempted in the desert for forty days by the devil (Matthew 4:1–11; Luke 4:1–13). His forty days here are clearly intended to be an echo of Israel's forty years in the wilderness. The difference is that, unlike us, Jesus is faithful. Our hope is not in our faithfulness, but in his. He's the representative of his people and he has passed the test. We can pray, 'Lead us not into temptation, but deliver us from the evil one', because Jesus has resisted temptation and resisted the evil one. Our victory and confidence are in him.

And it wasn't just God who tested Israel. Israel also tested God (Exodus 17:2, 7; Numbers 14:22; Psalms 78:41, 56; 95:8–9; 106:14). Jesus alludes to this in his confrontation with Satan in the wilderness. When Satan invites Jesus to precipitate the miraculous intervention of God, Jesus responds, 'It is also written: "Do not put the Lord your God to the test"' (Matthew 4:7; Luke 4:12). This is a quote from Deuteronomy 6:16 which says, 'Do not put the LORD your God to the test as you did at Massah.' Massah was where Israel tested God by grumbling about a lack of water. And this is the story that Psalm 95 recalls which is, in turn, the psalm quoted in Hebrews 3 – 4. The warning of Hebrews not to fall away is a warning not to test God by doubting his provision as a gracious and sovereign Father. 'Test' in 'Do not put the Lord your God to the test' is the same word as 'temptation' in the Lord's Prayer. We're not so much praying that we might not be tested, but that we might not test God. So Jesus is saying, 'Lead us not into the test of testing God. Don't let us be tempted to doubt God's provision as a gracious and sovereign Father.'

> **Reflection**
>
> Consider how you might use the Lord's Prayer as a
> framework for praying for different situations. For example,
> here's how you might use it to commit your day at work to
> God:
>
> > Our Father in heaven,
> > may my life today bring glory to your name.
> > Give me opportunities to extend your kingdom by speaking
> > > of Christ.
> > Help me to do your will and work with Christ as my boss.
> > Thank you for providing my job and please give me what I
> > > need to do it well.
> > Forgive my sins and help me to be patient with my
> > > colleagues.
> > Help me to not be shaped by the culture at work. Amen.

The exodus of Jesus shapes our prayers

One of the most striking things about the Lord's Prayer is how
much it's shaped by the story of the exodus.

Our Father in heaven. The story of the exodus is the first time
God describes his people as his son. 'Then say to Pharaoh,
"This is what the LORD says: Israel is my firstborn son, and
I told you, 'Let my son go, so that he may worship me.' But
you refused to let him go; so I will kill your firstborn son"'
(Exodus 4:22–23). To pray 'our Father' is to remember that
we're children of the liberating Father.

Hallowed be your name. At the burning bush, when God first
calls Moses to lead the Israelites out of slavery, Moses asks
how he should respond when the Israelites ask, 'What is

his name?' God responds by revealing his covenant name:
'I AM WHO I AM.' God is Yahweh, the LORD. 'This is my name
for ever, the name you shall call me from generation to
generation' (Exodus 3:13–15). Then, when Moses first goes
to Pharaoh, Pharaoh says, 'Who is the LORD, that I should
obey him and let Israel go? I do not know the LORD and I
will not let Israel go' (Exodus 5:2). The exodus becomes an
answer to the question: 'Who is the LORD?' God says to
Pharaoh, 'For by now I could have stretched out my hand
and struck you and your people with a plague that would
have wiped you off the earth. But I have raised you up for
this very purpose, that I might show you my power and that
my name might be proclaimed in all the earth' (Exodus
9:15–16; see also 7:5; 14:4).

Your kingdom come, your will be done. The exodus is set up as
a showdown between the kingdom of Pharaoh and the
kingdom of God, and between the gods of Egypt and the
living God. After the rescue through the Red Sea, Miriam
sings a song of praise that ends: 'The LORD reigns for ever
and ever' (Exodus 15:18). Israel's first theological reflection
on the exodus comes to the conclusion that God's kingdom
lasts for ever.

Give us today our daily bread. Once they were free from
Egypt, God provided manna for his people in the
wilderness, a bread from heaven (Exodus 16). Daily bread.
They could only gather enough for one day at a time, for a
day after the bread would turn mouldy. So each day, they
had to trust that God would provide for the following day.

Forgive us our debts, as we also have forgiven our debtors. God
led Israel to Mount Sinai where he made a covenant with

them. They would be his people, and he would be their
God. He gave his law to shape their life so that they would
be a witness to nations, revealing the goodness of his rule to
the world (Exodus 19:4–6; Deuteronomy 4:5–8). He gave
them the tabernacle as a model of forgiveness through
sacrifice. We've already seen how the Lord's Prayer echoes
the jubilee legislation of that covenant. Israel was liberated
to be a liberating people.

Lead us not into temptation. Again we've seen how this echoes
the next step in the story, namely the temptation of Israel
in the wilderness. Israel was tested by God, and Israel tested
God.

The point of these parallels is this: Jesus is about to achieve a
new exodus and create a new people. This is an exodus prayer,
a prayer for a new exodus and for a new exodus people. A
prayer that we might live as God's liberated people. We're
praying that:

- We might be the holy nation who makes God's holy
  name known to the nations.
- We might be the priestly kingdom which demonstrates
  the goodness of God's rule.
- We might trust God's daily provision so we are liberated
  to seek first his kingdom.
- We might be a jubilee community whose life reflects the
  mercy we've received.
- We might finally pass through temptation to enter
  God's promised rest because we're faithful in Christ.

All this we affirm and pray as we say, 'Our Father in heaven . . .',
because Jesus is achieving a new exodus. Matthew's Gospel is

structured around five blocks of teaching by Jesus, which may be a deliberate echo of the Pentateuch, the five books of Moses. The Lord's Prayer is given in the Sermon on the Mount. Just as Moses went up on a mountain to receive the old covenant, so Jesus is on a mountain teaching his new-covenant community about their new life. In Luke's Gospel, Jesus has already been transfigured on a mountain where he meets with Moses and Elijah and talks about 'his departure', literally 'his exodus' (Luke 9:28–31). Jesus is about to rescue his people from the slavery of sin and death. He will do so through a new passover. He himself is the Passover Lamb, for he will die in the place of his people.

So it's not surprising that the prayer is also echoed in the passion of Jesus. Facing the prospect of his crucifixion, Jesus prays in Gethsemane, 'Your will be done' (Matthew 26:42), a word-for-word repeat of the Lord's Prayer. As the Romans crucify him, he says, 'Father, forgive them, for they do not know what they are doing' (Luke 23:34), an echo of 'we also forgive everyone who sins against us'. He hangs under a sign reading: 'THIS IS JESUS, THE KING OF THE JEWS' (Matthew 27:37). His kingship and sonship are mocked (Matthew 27:42–43). In Gethsemane, he prays, 'My Father' (Matthew 26:39), but as the darkness of judgment comes over the cross, he feels forsaken by God (Matthew 27:46). Only at the end does he cry, 'Father, into your hands I commit my spirit' (Luke 23:46).

It's the cross that enables us to pray this prayer. Jesus loses his sense of sonship so that we might call God 'our Father'. We can entrust ourselves to God's will because God, in the person of his Son, put our needs before his desires, submitting to the will of the Father, and that will was our salvation. We can forgive because we've been forgiven through the cross. Every crime committed against us is judged, either at the last judgment or at the cross. Justice is done. Jesus was thirsty, so we can feast on him (John 19:28). We need not fear temptation or the evil one, because Jesus was faithful to the end, and Satan has been defeated. We can entrust ourselves to God, just as Jesus did. We can know God will hear our prayers and do what is good to us, even when we go through difficult times, because God has already demonstrated his love to us on the cross. Romans 8:32 says, 'He who did not spare his own Son, but gave him up for us all – how will he not also, along with him, graciously give us all things?'

The kingdom, the power and the glory

The line: 'For yours is the kingdom, the power and the glory for ever' isn't in the earliest manuscripts. It seems it was a later addition. But it's a fitting climax to the prayer, for it's a good summary of the concerns of the prayer, a prayer for God's glory ('hallowed be your name'), his kingdom ('your kingdom come') and his power ('give us . . . and forgive us . . .').

The Lord's Prayer is a short prayer, given as an alternative to long prayers. But it's also a big prayer, given as an alternative to small prayers. Throughout our exploration of this prayer, we've seen how it changes us. This is a big prayer that expands the lives of all who meaningfully pray it. By a big prayer, I don't mean a prayer with extravagant requests. Rather, prayers reaching far beyond me – prayers that have God and his glory at their centre. Goldfish grow to fill the space in which they're placed. If you put them in a small bowl, they'll remain small. But put them in a large tank, and they'll grow large. It's the same with Christians. We grow to fill the space created by our prayers. Truly pray the Lord's Prayer every day and you will grow to fill it.

Above all, the Lord's Prayer expands our view of God. The God of heaven is 'our Father' and he delights to hear his children pray. In Luke's Gospel, Jesus continues with this exhortation and encouragement: 'Ask and it will be given to you; seek and you will find; knock and the door will be opened to you. For everyone who asks receives; the one who seeks finds; and to the one who knocks, the door will be opened' (11:9–10). That's the simple invitation and exhortation that Jesus gives: Ask. Ask your heavenly Father. Ask, trusting that he will answer in his love.

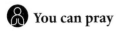 **You can pray**

The Lord's Prayer (based on Matthew 6:9–13 and Luke 11:2–4)

> Our Father in heaven,
> hallowed be your name.
> Your kingdom come,
> your will be done on earth as in heaven.
> Give us today our daily bread.
> Forgive us our sins,
> as we forgive those who sin against us.
> Lead us not into temptation,
> but deliver us from evil.
> For the kingdom, the power and the glory are yours.
> Now and for ever. Amen.

NOTES

Introduction

1. www.timchester.co.uk.

Chapter 1 The Father loves to hear us pray

1. See I. Howard Marshall, *The Gospel of Luke*, NIGTC (Eerdmans, 1978), p. 465, and M. M. B. Turner, 'Prayer in the Gospels and Acts', in D. A. Carson (ed.), *Teach Us to Pray: Prayer in the Bible and the World* (Baker/Paternoster, 1990), pp. 66–67.

2. Paul Miller, *A Praying Life: Connecting with God in a Distracting World* (NavPress, 2009), p. 133.

Chapter 2 The Son makes every prayer pleasing to God

1. Based on Friedrich Heiler, *Prayer: A Study in the History and Psychology of Religion* (Oxford University Press, 1937).

Chapter 3 The Spirit helps us as we pray

1. John Bunyan, *Praying in the Spirit* (1662), published in John Bunyan, *Prayer* (Banner of Truth, 1965), pp. 23, 27, 31, 32.

2. Bunyan, *Prayer*, p. 28.
3. Bunyan, *Prayer*, p. 33.
4. Douglas Moo, *The Epistle to the Romans*, NICNT (Eerdmans, 1996), p. 523.
5. Cited in Eric J. Alexander, *Prayer: A Biblical Perspective* (Banner of Truth, 2012), p. 71.

Chapter 4 'I've got more enjoyable things to do'

1. James B. Torrance, 'Christ in Our Place: The Joy of Worship', in Gerrit Dawson and Jock Stein (eds.), *A Passion for Christ: The Vision That Ignites Ministry* (Handsel, 1999), p. 51.
2. See www.three-two-one.org.
3. John Calvin, 'The Catechism of the Church of Geneva (1545)', *Theological Treatises*, Library of Christian Classics, vol. XXII, ed. J. K. S. Reid (Westminster Press/SCM, 1954), p. 122.

Chapter 5 'I've got more urgent things to do'

1. Thomas Goodwin, *The Return of Prayers* (Baker, 1839, 1979), p. 3.
2. This approach is sometimes called 'open theism'. See, for example, Clark Pinnock et al., *The Openness of God: A Biblical Challenge to the Traditional Understanding of God* (IVP Academic, 1994) and Clark Pinnock, *Most Moved Mover* (Baker, 2001). For a response to open theism, see Gerald Bray, *The Personal God: Is the Classical Understanding of God Tenable?* (Paternoster, 1998); John Frame, *No Other God: A Response to Open Theism* (P&R, 2001); Tony Gray and Chris Sinkinson, *Reconstructing Theology: A Critical Assessment of the Theology of Clark Pinnock* (Paternoster, 2000); John Piper, Justin Taylor and Paul Kjoss Helseth, *Beyond the Bounds: Open Theism and the Undermining of Biblical Christianity* (Crossway, 2003); Bruce Ware, *God's Lesser Glory: A Critique of Open Theism* (Apollos, 2001).

3. S. D. Gordon, *Quiet Talks on Prayer* (Marshall Pickering, 1904, 1984), p. 36.

4. Cited in J. Oswald Sanders, *Spiritual Leadership* (Moody, 1978), p. 83.

5. P. T. Forsyth, *The Soul of Prayer* (Independent Press, 1916, 1949), pp. 14, 57–58, 87.

6. Paul Miller, *A Praying Life: Connecting with God in a Distracting World* (NavPress, 2009), pp. 56, 66.

Chapter 6 'When I needed him, God didn't answer'

1. Charles Spurgeon, *The Treasury of David*, vol. 5 (Marshall, undated), p. 405, comment on Psalm 119:145. (Often attributed to Thomas Brooks.)

2. See Horatius Bonar, *God's Way of Holiness* (Evangelical Press, 1864, 1979), pp. 5–6.

3. D. A. Carson, *A Call to Spiritual Reformation: Priorities from Paul and His Prayers* (Baker/IVP, 1992), p. 158.

4. Matt Chandler, sermon on Romans 8:28–39, The Crowded House, Sheffield, 3 March 2013.

5. http://vimeo.com/63554398.

6. http://www.mattknellupdates.blogspot.co.uk/2013/06/matts-letter-to-fact.html.

Chapter 7 The battle to pray – and how to win it

1. John Stott, *Authentic Christianity*, ed. Timothy Dudley-Smith (IVP, 1995), pp. 225–226.

2. D. A. Carson, *A Call to Spiritual Reformation: Priorities from Paul and His Prayers* (Baker/IVP, 1992), p. 19.

3. Cited in Joel Beeke, 'Cultivating Private Prayer as a Pastor', Desiring God Conference for Pastors, 31 January 2011.

4. Marcus Honeysett, 'Bible Enjoyed', marcushoneysett. squarespace.com, 11 April 2009, http://marcushoneysett. squarespace.com/blog/bible-enjoyed-1.html.

5. Adapted from Kevin DeYoung, 'How to Pray Using Scripture', thegospelcoalition.org, 4 January 2013, http:// thegospelcoalition.org/blogs/kevindeyoung/2013/01/04/ how-to-pray-using-scripture.

6. Cited in Alister E. McGrath, *Christian Spirituality: An Introduction* (Blackwell, 1999), p. 87.

7. John Calvin, *The Institutes of Christian Religion*, Library of Christian Classics, vols. XX and XXI, tr. F. L. Battles, ed. J. T. McNeill (Westminster Press/SCM, 1961), the title of III.20.

8. John Bunyan, *Praying in the Spirit* (1662), published in John Bunyan, *Prayer* (Banner of Truth, 1965), p. 20.

9. Carson, *A Call to Spiritual Reformation*, p. 37.

Chapter 8 The arguments of prayer

1. Stuart Olyott, *Dare to Stand Alone* (Evangelical Press, 1982), p. 119.

2. John Bunyan, *Praying in the Spirit* (1662), published in John Bunyan, *Prayer* (Banner of Truth, 1965), p. 20.

3. William Gurnall, *The Christian in Complete Armour*, vol. 2 (Blackie & Son, 1865), p. 88.

Porterbrook Learning is a theological training course suitable for all Christians. It connects the heart and mission to the Bible story.

24 online modules to choose from, covering:
- Bible and Doctrine
- Character
- Church
- World

Join a Learning Site near you and enjoy:
- 4 conference days a year
- Presentation of your short unassessed assignments in tutorials at conference days
- Attendance at local Study Group meetings

....

'Affordable, high-quality training for mission and ministry in the 21st century. I warmly recommend it.'

Tim Keller, Senior Pastor, Redeemer Presbyterian Church, NY

....

Porterbrook Seminary
- Bible college-level programme of study
- Integrate theological training with uninterrupted involvement in ministry
- 10-15 hours of study per week
- Course taught through residential weeks, seminar days and guided reading

....

www.porterbrooknetwork.org
For news and offers on courses please visit:
www.facebook.com/Porterbrook.Network

Founders: Tim Chester and Steve Timmis